MCKINLEY LIBRARY
601 ALHAMBRA BOULEVARD
SACRAMENTO, CA 95816

12/99

WILDERNESS
NAVIGATION

WILDERNESS NAVIGATION

FINDING YOUR WAY USING MAP, COMPASS, ALTIMETER, & GPS

BOB BURNS
MIKE BURNS

THE
MOUNTAINEERS

*This book is dedicated to the memories of the teachers of navigation who
have gone before us, including Clinton M. Kelley, Richard B. Kaylor,
and Scott Fisher. Without their knowledge and leadership
some of us would still be lost in the wilderness.*

———————————

 Published by
The Mountaineers
1001 SW Klickitat Way, Suite 201
Seattle, WA 98134

First edition, 1999

Published simultaneously in Great Britain by Cordee, 3a DeMontfort Street,
Leicester, England, LE1 7HD

Manufactured in Canada

Edited by Paul Hughes
Illustrations by Gray Mouse Graphics unless otherwise noted
Cover and book design by Jennifer Shontz
Layout by Jennifer Shontz

Cover photograph: Jim Fagiolo; Back cover photos: William G. Garcia

Library of Congress Cataloging-in-Publication Data
Burns, Bob, 1942–
    Wilderness navigation: finding your way using map, compass,
    altimeter, and GPS / Bob Burns, Mike Burns; [edited by Paul Hughes;
    illustrations by Gray Mouse Graphics unless otherwise noted].—
    1st ed.
        p.   cm.
    Includes bibliographical references (p.) and index.
    ISBN 0-89886-629-4
    1. Orienteering—Equipment and supplies. 2. Navigation—Equipment
and supplies. 3. Outdoor recreation—Equipment and supplies.
I. Burns, Mike, 1970–   . II. Hughes, Paul. III. Title.
GV200.4.B87 1998
796.58—dc21   98-49711
                                                                  CIP

TABLE of CONTENTS

PREFACE AND ACKNOWLEDGMENTS

The origins of this book are lost among the rough notes of The Mountaineers' first climbing course, held over sixty years ago. These notes were eventually published as the *Mountaineers Handbook* in 1948. But time and technology changed wilderness travel and mountain climbing, and as a result a new book, *Mountaineering: The Freedom of the Hills*, was published in 1960. This is a comprehensive book, containing information on equipment, navigation, wilderness travel, and technical details of climbing on rock, snow, and glaciers.

Ever since the first edition of *Freedom*, revision committees have repeatedly been formed to study the state of the art of wilderness travel and climbing, survey the market for equipment, and revise the book. These efforts resulted in the second through the sixth editions of *Freedom* in 1967, 1974, 1982, 1992, and 1997. More revisions are anticipated in the future. The elder of the two authors was part of the past three revision committees, responsible for the chapter on navigation. The younger author also worked on the sixth edition, providing material for the navigation, leadership, and safety chapters.

In addition to writing about navigation, both of the authors have hiked, scrambled, snowshoed, and climbed extensively for many years. They have also been actively involved with teaching wilderness navigation, predominantly in climbing courses but also as part of The Mountaineers' snowshoeing and alpine scrambling courses. They have also taught navigation in special map and compass seminars sponsored by the Club, and in some forums outside the Club as well. In some of the non-climbing classes, they have frequently been asked to recommend a book covering the material presented in their courses and lectures. Though there are many fine books on the subject of map and compass usage, the only book using the same methods and covering the same material as these courses is *Freedom*. Many students in ski, snowshoe, and hiking activities balk at buying a large, relatively expensive book filled with all the details of technical rock and ice climbing just to obtain information on wilderness navigation. It is out of this need that the idea for *Wilderness Navigation* emerged.

The original concept for this book was merely to publish the navigation chapter from the sixth edition of *Freedom* as a small booklet, for use by non-climbers, assuming that anyone interested in technical climbing would buy *Freedom*. Though written for climbers, the material in that chapter is equally applicable to all wilderness travelers, including hikers, scramblers, snowshoers, cross-country skiers, forest workers, and others. Accordingly, the title of *Wilderness Navigation* was chosen, to emphasize the fact that its intended audience is anyone who ventures off the road and into the wilderness—any area away from roads and the conveniences of the modern world.

The temptation to expand on the material covered in *Freedom*, however, was irresistible. Though *Wilderness Navigation* is intended to be a small, affordable book focused on wilderness navigation, we also recognized that much additional information on the subject had been excluded from *Freedom* in order to keep its size manageable. (Even with the effort to limit its size, *Freedom 6* ended up being over 500 pages in length!) Freed from such restrictions, *Wilderness Navigation* was expanded, by adding technical information on ascertaining the grade and direction, or bearing, of a slope on a map; clinometer usage; the use of the bearing of a slope in orientation; information regarding changing declination; a world declination map; additional tips on how to avoid getting lost; added emphasis on awareness of topography in orientation and navigation; and details on how to use the Global Positioning System (GPS) in wilderness navigation, utilizing techniques not mentioned in most GPS receiver instruction manuals. Material on the subject of wilderness routefinding was also added, as well as an appendix with thirty practice problems. The result is still a small, focused, affordable book, but it contains over twice as much material as the navigation chapter in *Freedom 6*. Since much of the added information (such as slope grade and bearing) is applicable to climbers as well as others, this book should also be useful to climbers.

The methods of compass usage in this book have been taught for many years by The Mountaineers and are consistent with those pioneered by the Silva Company and adapted by Suunto, Nexus, and Brunton. Readers who purchase base plate compasses from any of these suppliers will find the *Wilderness Navigation* compass usage methods consistent with those given in their compass instruction manuals (though the methods presented here offer a slight modification to make compass use even easier with some compasses). When using the methods explained in this book, orienting the map is not necessary, nor is it necessary to draw declination lines on your maps, in order to use the map and compass together. Instead, we explain how to make *all* compasses work like "set and forget" compasses with adjustable declination arrows. This has proven to be a dependable and easy-to-learn method of dealing with declination.

ACKNOWLEDGMENTS

The authors wish to express their appreciation to a number of organizations and individuals who have contributed significantly to this book. First, we would like to thank Dr. C. E. Barton of the Australian Geological Survey Organisation, who created the world declination map that appears here as Figure 9 and gave us permission to reproduce it, as well as the International Association of Geomagnetism and Aeronomy (IAGA), which created the computer model of the earth's magnetic field on which the declination map is based, and Larry Newitt of the Geological Survey of Canada, whose work with the Canadian Geomagnetic Reference Field we used to create the declination map of the United States. In addition, we are grateful to our friend Ronald Gailis for his help in navigating through the World Wide Web in search of sites for information on geomagnetism.

We also wish to express our most sincere appreciation to the staff of The Mountaineers Books, particularly to Margaret Foster, for bringing our vision to life. Extra special thanks to our friend Steve Cox for his continuing support, advice, encouragement, and behind-the-scenes work that made this book possible.

INTRODUCTION

Where am I? How can I find my way from here to there? How far is it to my destination? Will I be able to find my way back? These are some of the most frequently asked questions in wilderness travel, and this book shows how to find the answers by using orientation and navigation.

By the time you finish this book, you will have a good handle on the tools of navigation and the proven techniques of top-notch navigators, acquired through years of roaming (and being lost in) the wilderness. You will have the basic knowledge to head into the wilds, work out the way to your destination, and, most importantly, find your way home.

These tools and techniques are simple and straightforward—but exacting. Study them carefully to help make your wilderness adventures successful and keep you safe and within the ranks of surviving navigators. Before you immerse yourself in this book, remember two things: navigation is easy, and navigation is fun. (So much fun, in fact, that some people engage in the sport of *orienteering*, in which the participants compete with one another over a structured course, getting to various destinations using map and compass.)

First, a few definitions:

Orientation is the science of determining your exact position on the earth. People who spend a reasonable amount of time and effort usually gain these skills, even if they have little background or interest in math or science.

Navigation is the science of determining the location of your objective and of keeping yourself pointed in the right direction from your starting point to this destination. Like orientation, navigation is a required skill for all wilderness travelers.

Routefinding is the art of selecting and following the best path appropriate for the abilities and equipment of the party. It takes a lot to be a good routefinder: an integrated sense of terrain and a combination of good judgment, experience, acute awareness, and instinct. In addition to a solid foundation in the orientation and navigation skills described in the following chapters, wilderness routefinding also requires considerable time, practice, and experience.

The route through this book is divided into two parts. The first, consisting of chapters 1 through 4, contains information on maps, compasses, orientation, how to avoid getting lost, and what to do if you *do* get lost. These chapters are essential to all outdoor travelers who wish to become adept at map and compass usage: hikers, scramblers, skiers, snowshoers, mountain climbers, and any other sporting enthusiasts who venture off the road and into the wilderness, and also those who never intend to leave a well-maintained trail.

Chapters 5 through 8 provide information on off-trail wilderness navigation, the use of altimeters and GPS receivers, and wilderness routefinding on trails, in the forest, in alpine areas, and on snow and glaciers. We recommend a careful reading of these chapters for anyone who intends to leave the trail and venture cross-country in search of hidden fishing lakes, challenging mountain peaks, interesting cross-country ski routes, and other destinations that cannot be reached by following a well-maintained trail.

As you read this book, you should have a map and a compass handy and follow along with the examples given in the text. Navigation is not a passive activity; it requires getting involved and using your brain.

After reading this book, you will probably *not* be an expert in wilderness navigation. Only practice and a lot of experience will enable you to become an expert. But this book *can* give you a basic foundation in the skills necessary for safe and enjoyable wilderness travel.

We remind the reader that this is a book about *orientation, navigation,* and *routefinding.* It is *not* a book about how to climb steep snow, how to travel safely in avalanche-prone areas, how to climb technical rock, or how to travel in safety on glaciers. Doing any of these activities requires that the traveler take courses and have considerable practice in the necessary techniques, under the tutelage of experienced and qualified individuals or groups. The bibliography at the end of this book suggests some publications covering these subjects. We urge the reader to study and practice such subjects carefully before undertaking any potentially hazardous travel.

THE MAP

A map is a symbolic picture of a place. In convenient shorthand, it conveys a phenomenal amount of information in a form that is easy to understand and easy to carry. No one should venture into the wilderness without a map of the area, or without the skills required to interpret and thoroughly understand it. Note the publication date of the map because roads, trails, and other features may have changed since that time. Try to use the latest information. Several different types of maps are available:

Relief maps attempt to show terrain in three dimensions by using various shades of green, gray, and brown, terrain sketching, and raised surfaces. They help in visualizing the ups and downs of the landscape and have some value in trip planning.

Land management and recreation maps are frequently updated and thus are very useful for current details on roads, trails, ranger stations, and other marks of the human hand. They usually show only the horizontal relationship of natural features, without the contour lines that indicate the shape of the land. These maps, published by the U.S. Forest Service, National Park Service, other government agencies, and timber companies, are suitable for trip planning.

Sketch maps tend to be crudely drawn but often make up in specialized route detail what they lack in draftsmanship. Such drawings can be effective supplements to other map and guidebook information.

Guidebook maps vary greatly in quality. Some are merely sketches, while others are accurate modifications of topographic maps. They often contain useful details on roads, trails, and wilderness routes.

Topographic maps are the best of all for wilderness travelers. They depict topography, the shape of the earth's surface, by showing contour lines that represent constant elevations above and below sea level. These maps, essential to off-trail travel, are produced in many countries. Some are produced by government agencies, such as the U.S. Geological Survey (USGS), whereas others are printed by private companies. Some private companies produce maps based on USGS maps, but updated with recent trail and road details and sometimes combine sections of USGS maps. These maps are often useful supplements to standard topographic maps and are particularly useful in trail hiking. As an example of topographic maps, we will look in detail at USGS maps.

USGS TOPOGRAPHIC MAPS

It might be interesting to start this discussion of USGS maps with a refresher on how cartographers divide up the earth. The distance around our planet is divided into 360 units called *degrees*. A measurement east or west is called *longitude*. A measurement north or south is *latitude*. Longitude is measured from zero to 180 degrees, both east and west, starting at the Greenwich meridian in England. Latitude is measured from zero to 90 degrees, north and south, from the equator. New York City, for example, is situated at 74 degrees west longitude and 41 degrees north latitude (74° W and 41° N).

Each degree is divided into sixty units called *minutes*, and each minute is further subdivided into sixty *seconds*. On a map, a latitude of 46 degrees, 53 minutes, and 15 seconds north would be written like this: 46°53′15″ N.

One type of USGS map commonly used by wilderness travelers covers an area of 7.5 minutes (that is, ⅛ degree) of latitude by 7.5 minutes of longitude. These maps are known as the *7.5-minute series*. An older type of USGS map covers an area of 15 minutes (that is, ¼ degree) of latitude by 15 minutes of longitude. These maps are part of what is called the *15-minute series*.

The *scale* of a map is a ratio between measurements on the map and measurements in the real world. A common way to state the scale is to compare a map measurement with a ground measurement (as in 1 inch equals 1 mile) or to give a specific mathematical ratio (as in 1:24,000, where any one unit of measure on the map equals 24,000 units of the same measure on the earth). The scale is usually shown graphically at the bottom of the map.

In the USGS 7.5-minute series, the scale is 1:24,000, or roughly

2.5 inches to the mile, or 4 centimeters (cm) to the kilometer (km). Each map covers an area of approximately 6 by 9 miles, or 9 by 14 km. In the 15-minute series, the scale is 1:62,500, or about 1 inch to 1 mile (1.6 cm to 1 km), and each map covers an area of about 12 by 18 miles, or 18 by 28 km. Off-trail travelers prefer the 7.5-minute maps because of the greater detail.

The 7.5-minute map is now the standard for the United States, except for Alaska. The 15-minute maps are no longer in production for the other forty-nine states. For Alaska only, the 15-minute map is still the standard, and the scale is somewhat different: 1:63,360, or exactly 1 inch to the mile. The east-west extent of each Alaska map is actually greater than 15 minutes because of the way in which the lines of longitude converge towards the North Pole.

How to Read Topographic Maps

Consider this a language lesson, but a map's language is easy to learn and pays immediate rewards to any wilderness traveler. Some of this language is in words, but most of it is in the form of symbols. The best way to follow the lesson is to study it along with an actual USGS topographic map. We suggest you now get a topographic map. Any map will do.

Each map is referred to as a quadrangle (or quad) and covers an area bounded on the north and south by latitude lines that differ by an amount equal to the map series (7.5 minutes or 15 minutes), and on the east and west by longitude lines that differ by the same amount. Each quadrangle is given the name of a prominent topographic or manmade feature of the area.

Declination Information and North-South Reference Lines

The margins of USGS maps hold important information, such as the date of publication and revision, the names of maps of adjacent areas, contour intervals, and map scales. The margin also gives the area's magnetic declination, which is the difference between true north and magnetic north (declination is extremely important and we will discuss it in chapter 2 of this book). Topographic maps older than 1989 usually have a declination diagram printed near the lower left-hand corner of the map. The "star" indicates true north and the "MN" indicates the direction to magnetic north. The difference between these two is the magnetic declination. Maps printed in 1989 or later usually do not have declination diagrams, but instead have a statement such as "1989 magnetic declination 19°30′ EAST." Since there are sixty minutes

(60') in a degree, this means that the declination is 19.5 degrees east.

Depending on the map's date of revision, there may or may not be UTM (Universal Transverse Mercator) lines printed on the map. Maps printed in 1989 or later usually have a grid of black lines representing 1000-meter intervals of the UTM grid. This grid is usually slightly offset from true north. The amount of this offset is given by a statement in the lower left corner of the map such as "UTM GRID DECLINATION. . . . 0°14' WEST." These lines may be used as a north-south reference, as explained in chapter 2 of this book, but only if the offset of the grid is less than one degree. If the offset of the UTM grid is more than one degree, then you should use surveyors' section lines (usually printed in red). If the area has not been surveyed, or if the section lines do not truly run north-south, then you should draw in your own north-south lines. Put your map on a table and lay one long edge of a yardstick along the left margin of the map. Draw a line along the other side of the yardstick, then move the yardstick over to the line you have just drawn and draw another line, and another, and so on until you reach the center of the map. Then place the yardstick along the right margin of the map and repeat the procedure. This way, you will have a set of north-south lines that are truly north-south. This will help you achieve accuracy in measuring and plotting bearings on the map using your compass.

On maps printed prior to 1989, UTM lines are usually not shown. However, there are faint tick marks along the edges of such maps showing the locations of the 1000-meter lines. The declination diagrams for these maps usually have a line to *GN*, meaning "grid north." This is the offset of the UTM grid from true north. If this offset is less than one degree, then you can connect these lines on your table at home using a yardstick to place a UTM grid on the map. You can then use these as north-south reference lines. However, if the amount of difference between true north and grid north is greater than one degree, then you should draw in your own north-south lines parallel with the edges of the map, as described earlier.

What the Colors Mean

Colors on a USGS topographic map have specific meanings. This is what the different colors stand for:

Red: Major roads and survey information.

Blue: Rivers, lakes, springs, waterfalls, and other water-related features.

Black: Minor roads, trails, railroads, buildings, bench marks, latitude and longitude lines, UTM coordinates and lines, and other features not part of the natural environment.

Green: Areas of heavy forest. Solid green marks a forested area, while mottled green indicates scrub vegetation. A lack of green does not mean an area is devoid of vegetation but simply that any growth is too small or scattered to show on the map. You should not be surprised if a small, narrow gully with no green color on the map turns out to be an avalanche gully, choked with impassable brush in the summer and fall and posing a significant avalanche hazard in the winter and spring.

White: The color of the paper on which the map is printed; it can have a variety of meanings, depending on the terrain.

White with blue contour lines: A glacier or permanent snowfield. The contour lines of glaciers and permanent snowfields are in solid blue, with their edges indicated by dashed blue lines. Elevations are shown in blue. *Rope up* for all glacier travel!

White with brown contour lines: Any area without substantial forest, such as a high alpine area, a clear-cut, a rock slide, an avalanche gully, or a meadow. Study the map for other clues.

Brown: Contour lines and elevations, everywhere except on glaciers and permanent snowfields.

Purple: Partial revision of an existing map.

Translating Contour Lines

The heart of a topographic map is its overlay of contour lines, each line indicating a constant elevation as it follows the shape of the landscape. A map's contour interval is the difference in elevation between two adjacent contour lines. The contour interval is clearly printed at the bottom of the map. Every fifth contour line is printed darker than the other lines and is labeled with the elevation.

One of the most important bits of information a topographic map reveals is whether you will be traveling uphill or downhill. If the route crosses lines of increasingly higher elevation, you will be going uphill. If it crosses lines of decreasing elevation, the route is downhill. Flat or sidehill travel is indicated by a route that crosses no lines, remaining within a single contour interval.

Topographic maps also show cliffs, passes, summits, and other features (fig. 1). The following are the main features depicted by contour lines:

Flat areas: No contour lines at all.

Gentle slopes: Widely spaced contour lines.

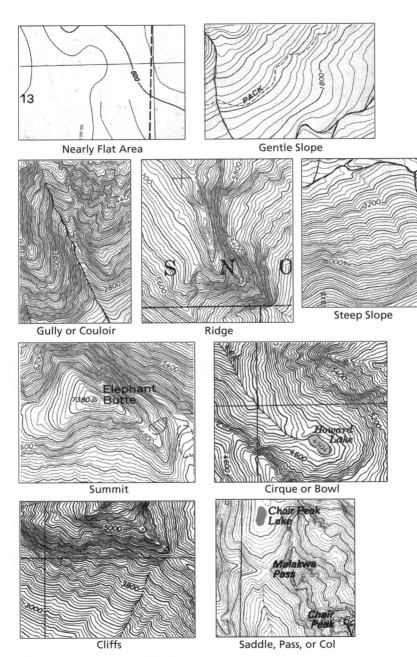

Figure 1. Basic topographic features

Steep slopes: Closely spaced contour lines.

Cliffs: Contour lines extremely close together or touching.

Valleys, ravines, gullies, and couloirs: Contour lines in a pattern of Us for gentle, rounded valleys or gullies; Vs for sharp valleys and gullies. The Us and Vs point uphill, in the direction of higher elevation.

Ridges or spurs: Contour lines in a pattern of Us for gentle, rounded ridges; Vs for sharp ridges. The Us and Vs point downhill, in the direction of lower elevation.

Peaks or summits: A concentric pattern of contour lines, with the summit being the innermost and highest ring. Peaks are also often indicated by Xs, elevations, bench marks (BMs), or a triangle symbol.

Cirques or bowls: Patterns of contour lines forming a semicircle (or as much as three-quarters of a circle), rising from a low spot in the center to form a natural amphitheater at the head of a valley.

Saddles, passes, or cols: An hourglass shape, with higher contour lines on two sides, indicating a low point on a ridge.

As you travel in the wilderness, you should frequently observe the terrain and its depiction on the map. Note all the topographic features—such as ridges, gullies, streams, and summits—as you pass them. This will help you to maintain a close estimate of exactly where you are and will help you become an expert map reader. You will get better and better at interpreting these lines by comparing actual terrain with its representation on the map (fig. 2). The goal is to someday glance at a topographic map and have a sharp mental image of just what the place will look like.

Distance Measurement on the Map

You can easily measure distances on the map using the scales at the bottom. To measure a straight-line distance, simply measure the length of the line on the map using the inch or millimeter scale of your compass. Then transfer this distance to one of the scales at the bottom of the map and read off the number of feet, meters, or miles. If the distance on the map is greater than the length of your compass scale, or if the route is not a straight line, then you can use the lanyard attached to the compass instead. Put the free end of the lanyard on one point on the map, then place the lanyard on the route to be measured, curving it along the trail, ridge, or other feature, until it reaches the other point on the map. Then straighten out the lanyard and place it alongside the desired scale at the bottom of the map. While following trails with numerous short switchbacks, this

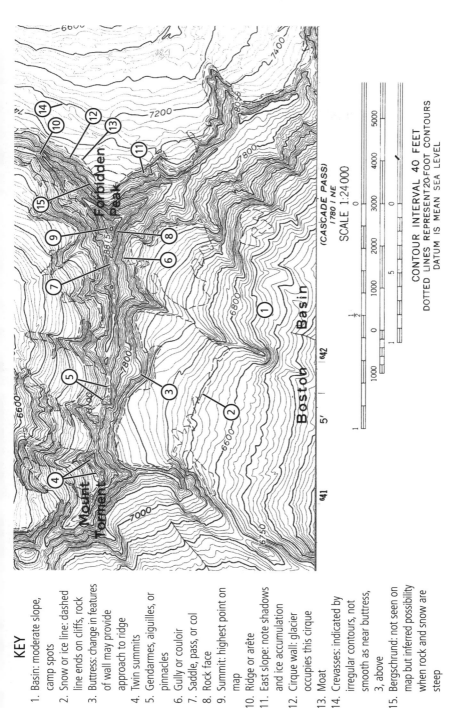

KEY

1. Basin: moderate slope, camp spots
2. Snow or ice line: dashed line ends on cliffs, rock
3. Buttress: change in features of wall may provide approach to ridge
4. Twin summits
5. Gendarmes, aiguilles, or pinnacles
6. Gully or couloir
7. Saddle, pass, or col
8. Rock face
9. Summit: highest point on map
10. Ridge or arête
11. East slope: note shadows and ice accumulation
12. Cirque wall: glacier occupies this cirque
13. Moat
14. Crevasses: indicated by irregular contours, not smooth as near buttress, 3, above
15. Bergschrund: not seen on map but inferred possibility when rock and snow are steep

(CASCADE PASS)
1780 I NE

SCALE 1:24 000

CONTOUR INTERVAL 40 FEET
DOTTED LINES REPRESENT 20-FOOT CONTOURS
DATUM IS MEAN SEA LEVEL

Figure 2. Photograph of a mountainous area; keyed features are represented on the accompanying topographic map.

method will probably be quite inaccurate, since the lanyard may not be able to keep up with all the tiny zigzags. In this case, you may have to estimate an additional amount of distance depending on the number of switchbacks that you were not able to measure accurately. You can also buy a small map measuring instrument, although these are generally no more accurate than the lanyard method and add a slight, unnecessary weight. Because of this, we do not recommend such devices for most wilderness navigation.

You can use either feet and miles or meters and kilometers for measuring or pacing distances. However, the metric units are much easier to use, since you can easily convert distances from kilometers to meters and vice versa in your head, by multiplying or dividing by 1000. Converting from miles to feet or vice versa, on the other hand, requires multiplying or dividing by 5280 (the number of feet in a mile), which can be time-consuming and cumbersome in the field. Most wilderness travelers do not wish to carry pocket calculators on their adventures. Also, most countries in the world publish maps based solely on the metric system.

Pace. It is occasionally necessary to go a certain distance in a given direction, such as 100 meters or 1000 feet in a northeasterly direction. Doing this requires a good estimate of your *pace*. All wilderness travelers should have a good idea of the length of their pace. The length of your normal pace is the distance required to walk two steps (one with each foot) on level ground at a comfortable walking stride. To measure your normal pace, establish a starting point in an open area where you will be able to walk in a straight line on level terrain. Walk for ten full paces (ten steps with each foot). After taking these ten paces, mark the place where you stopped. Then measure that distance with a tape measure. This measurement can be in either feet or meters, whichever form of measurement you prefer. Divide this distance by the ten paces to get the length of your pace. The normal pace for most people ranges from 3 to 6 feet, or from 1 to 2 meters.

Once you know your pace, you can use it to travel a certain distance in the field. Suppose you want to travel 1000 feet, and you know your pace is 5 feet. Divide 1000 feet by 5 feet per pace, and the result is 200 paces. This is easy to do if the numbers are simple, as in this example. If the numbers do not divide evenly, such as when traveling 840 feet with a pace of 5.3 feet, you may need a calculator to figure out the number of paces. It is impractical to carry a calculator on a wilderness trek, so this sort of calculation is best done at home before the trip, as a part of making a route plan.

When using the length of pace in your travels, keep in mind that your actual stride will vary considerably due to differences in terrain. For example, your stride will be shorter when going uphill or through heavy brush and will probably be longer when descending a good trail. So whenever you use your pace in navigation, be sure to make allowances for variations in the length of your pace with the terrain.

Counting paces is a poor way to travel in the wilderness, since it is easy to lose count. If you concentrate hard enough to avoid losing count, you may then miss important details of the route, such as key topographic features, and it may detract from your enjoyment of the trip. Keeping track of your location is far better done by watching the topography. If counting paces is necessary at all, we recommend that you use it only for short distances.

Slope Measurement on the Map

By carefully measuring the distance between contour lines on a topographic map, you can estimate the steepness of the slope, or *grade*, in percent. This knowledge is important in deciding the feasibility of a particular route. You can do this in the field, but it is easiest if done at home before your trip in the wilderness.

Draw a line on the map indicating your proposed route. Pick out the place on this line that appears to be the steepest—the place where the contour lines are closest together. Identify two particular contour lines in this area—for example, the lines at 3000 feet and 3200 feet. The difference between these two lines is the vertical height of the slope—in this case, 200 feet. Now, measure the *horizontal* distance between these same two lines with the scale of your compass (or any other suitable device). Transfer this measurement to the feet scale at the bottom of the map. Suppose you get 400 feet. By knowing the vertical height and the horizontal distance, you can easily determine the *grade* of the slope, a measure of how steep it is. (Of course, you can use meters instead of feet if you wish, as long as you use the same units for both vertical and horizontal measurements.)

The grade is the vertical height divided by the horizontal distance, multiplied by 100%. Thus, if the vertical height is 200 feet and the horizontal distance is 400 feet, as in the above example, the grade is 50%. This is a steep slope, corresponding to about 27 degrees.

If the vertical height is equal to the horizontal distance, the grade is 100%, and the angle of the slope is 45 degrees.

Figure 3 shows several examples of measuring the grade of the slope. Points *A* and *B* are at elevations of 3600 and 3400 feet, so the vertical height is 3600 minus 3400, or 200 feet. The horizontal distance on the map, which can be measured with a ruler, is found to be 5 centimeters. Transferring this to the scale for feet at the bottom of the map gives a distance of 3800 feet. The grade is 200 feet divided by 3800 feet, times 100%, or 0.05 times 100%, which equals 5%.

Points *C* and *D* are at elevations of 5000 feet and 4600 feet, so the vertical height is 400 feet. The horizontal distance is 10 millimeters, which, when transferred to the scale for feet, gives 800 feet. The grade is 400 feet divided by 800 feet, times 100%, which equals 50%.

Points *E* and *F* are at elevations of 4800 feet and 4200 feet. The vertical height is 600 feet. The horizontal distance on the map is 8 millimeters, corresponding to a distance of 600 feet. This is the same as the vertical height of 600 feet, so the grade is 100%, or a 45-degree angle.

Measuring grade of the slope is easy; it merely requires dividing the vertical height by the horizontal distance. But expressing the result as an *angle*, in degrees, requires the use of trigonometry, which we would rather avoid in the field. For your information, the relationship between slope grade and slope angle is shown in the following table:

Slope Grade and Slope Angle			
% Grade	Angle (in degrees)	% Grade	Angle (in degrees)
0%	0°	120%	50°
20%	11°	140%	54°
40%	22°	160%	58°
50%	27°	180%	61°
60%	31°	200%	63°
80%	39°	250%	68°
100%	45°	300%	72°

You can use this table (or trigonometry if you know it) for trip planning at home, but in the field you usually only need to know two values: a 50% grade has an angle of 27 degrees, and a 100% grade has an angle of 45 degrees. These two numbers can help you to determine the feasibility of negotiating a particular slope and can

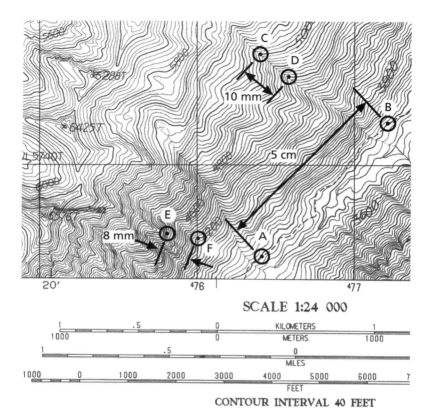

SCALE 1:24 000

CONTOUR INTERVAL 40 FEET

Figure 3. Measuring grade on a map *(Illustration by J. Shontz)*

also help you to assess the risk of avalanche hazard (see chapter 8). A 50% grade (27-degree angle) is quite a steep slope, near the limit for casual hiking. Slopes steeper than 50% can involve difficult scrambling or climbing. By the time the grade gets to 100% (a 45-degree angle), the terrain is usually too steep for unroped travel, and you will probably need to belay for safety. On snow, you may need an ice ax even if the grade is less than 50%.

All wilderness travelers should know their limits when it comes to slope. Sometime when you are going up or down a slope that appears to be at your limit, and you feel uncomfortable about being on steeper terrain, mark that spot on your map. Later, measure the grade of that slope as mentioned above. Then you will know your limit, and the next time you contemplate a route in unfamiliar territory, you will be able to measure its grade on the map and see if it is within your limits.

Direction of the Slope

Traveling along a contour line means traveling on a level route with no slope. Conversely, the direction perpendicular (at a right angle) to a contour line gives the direction of the slope—the direction directly uphill or downhill, sometimes called the "fall line." You can easily find this direction on the map or in the field for any point on sloping terrain. This fact can be very useful in orientation, and we will refer to it in several places in this book. For example, in figure 4, point G has a slope which falls off to the southwest. Point H, on the other hand, has a slope falling off roughly to the east. We will be able to express this direction more precisely after we explain how to measure and plot bearings using the compass in chapter 2.

Using the direction of the slope cannot prove that you are at any particular place, but it can disprove it, and this can sometimes be a big help in trying to figure out where you are. In figure 4, for example, suppose you have climbed Peak 6547 and have descended a few hundred feet. You wish to find out where you are, and you guess that you are at point G. That means that the slope should be falling off to the southwest. However, when standing on the slope and facing downhill, you see the midday sun on your right, so you know that you are facing roughly east. This proves that you cannot be at point G. You could very possibly be at point H, since the slope there falls off to the east. But there are other places where the slope falls off to the east, so you cannot prove that you are at point H.

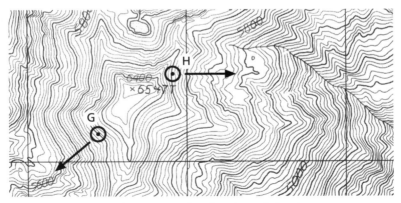

Figure 4. Examples of observing the direction of the slope on a map (Illustration by J. Shontz)

LIMITATIONS OF MAPS

Keep a couple of cautionary thoughts in mind as you study a topographic map. The map will not show all the terrain features you actually see on your trip because there is a limit to what map makers can jam onto the map without reducing it to an unreadable clutter. If a feature is not at least as high as the contour interval, it may not be shown, so a 30-foot cliff may come as a surprise when you are navigating with a map that has a 40-foot contour interval. Check the date of the map, because topographic maps are not revised very often, and information on forests and on roads and other works of the human hand could be out of date. A forest may have been logged or a road extended or closed since the last updating. Although topographic maps are essential to wilderness travel, you often need to supplement them with information from visitors to the area, guidebooks, and other maps. When you learn of changes, you should note them on your map.

CUSTOMIZING AND MODIFYING MAPS

Sometimes a trip runs through portions of two or more maps. Adjoining maps can be folded at the edges and brought together, or you can create your own customized map by cutting out the non-pertinent areas and splicing the rest together with tape. Include plenty of territory so that you will have a good overview of the entire trip, including the surrounding area (which might be needed for orientation, as explained in chapter 3). Black-and-white photocopies are good for marking the route, but since they do not show colors, they should be used only as supplements to the real thing. If a durable, high-quality reproduction is needed, then a color photocopy onto waterproof paper may be the best approach.

Some wilderness travelers cut off the white borders of their maps in order to minimize the amount of weight they carry. This practice is of questionable value, since these blank areas are useful for making notes regarding your trip, and the weight saved is so little. If you wish to do this, be careful not to cut off any of the very important information at the bottom of the map, such as the scales, date of the map, declination information, and contour interval. Some of the information at the lower left-hand corner of the map might not seem too important if you are not using GPS (see chapter 7). But if you ever decide to buy a GPS receiver, you may later regret having cut off and discarded essential information regarding the UTM zone and map datum.

CARRYING MAPS ON A WILDERNESS TRIP

As the precious objects they are, maps deserve tender care in the wilds. You can make a map more durable by laminating it with a plastic film or by giving it a waterproof coating. Some maps can be purchased already waterproofed. Such coatings, however, are difficult to mark on and make the map harder to work with and fold. A waterproof coating also makes a map more slippery, and more likely to slide down a snow slope if you drop it.

Many people carry their maps in a well-protected place such as in the top flaps of their packs. In doing so, they protect their maps from the elements, but at the same time they make it inconvenient to look at them, since they must remove their packs to do so. Instead of doing this, we suggest that you carry your map in a pocket or some other readily accessible place so you do not have to take off your pack to get at it. "Cargo" shorts with big pockets are excellent for carrying maps, compasses, and other objects that you want to have quickly and conveniently available. Elsewhere in this book we will point out the importance of making frequent observations of the map to aid you in orientation and navigation. Following this advice is a lot easier if it is possible to get at your map at any time.

One good way to carry a map is to fold it to show the area where you will be traveling, and then to enclose it in a clear plastic map case or a reclosable plastic sandwich bag. This way, it will be protected from the elements, always visible, easy to remove, and compact. If protected in this way, you can even glissade down a snow slope with the map in your back pocket without damaging it.

WHERE TO GET MAPS

Many outdoor recreation stores sell topographic maps, as do some bookstores and even some nautical supply stores. Look in the yellow pages of the telephone directory under "Maps, retail."

You can order maps directly from the USGS by calling 1-800-435-7627. The address is USGS, P.O. Box 25286, Denver, CO 80225. If you do not know the name of the map for the area you need, you can order a *Topographic Map Index Circular* for your state, as well as a booklet entitled *Topographic Maps*. These are free. The index circular shows the names of all the quadrangles in your state, so you can find which one(s) you need for any particular trip. Then you can order the maps directly from the USGS, following the instructions given on the index circular.

To obtain topographic maps for Canada, write to Canada Map Office, 615 Booth Street, Ottawa, Ontario K1A 0E9.

For special maps, such as those of state or national parks, you can contact the National Geographic Information Center, United States Geological Survey, 12201 Sunrise Valley Drive, Reston, VA 22092. The phone number is 1-800-USA-MAPS.

THE POWER OF THE MAP

With the exception of your brain, the topographic map is your most important navigational tool. No one should venture into the wilderness without one. The map gives you information about direction, the distance between any two points, the shape of the terrain, human and natural features, the amount of vegetation, the location of water features, the direction and grade of the slope, and more. But as useful as maps are by themselves, they become even more powerful when used with a compass.

THE COMPASS

The compass is a very simple device that can do a wondrous thing. It can reveal at any time and any place exactly what direction you are heading. On a simple wilderness trek in good weather, the compass may never leave your pack or pocket. But as the route becomes more complex or as the weather worsens, it comes into its own as a critical tool of wilderness travel.

A compass is nothing more than a magnetized needle that responds to the earth's magnetic field. Compass makers have added a few things to this basic unit to make it easier to use. But stripped to the core, there is just that needle, aligned with the earth's magnetism, and from that we can figure out any direction.

These are the basic features (fig. 5a) of a wilderness travel compass:

- A freely rotating magnetic needle—one end is a different color from the other so you can tell which end is pointing north.
- A circular, rotating housing, or capsule, for the needle—this is filled with a fluid that dampens (reduces) the vibrations of the needle, making readings more accurate.
- A dial around the circumference of the housing—the dial should be graduated clockwise from 0 to 360 degrees, in 2 degree increments.
- An orienting arrow and a set of parallel meridian lines—these are located below the needle.
- An index line—read bearings here.
- A transparent, rectangular base plate for the entire unit—this includes a direction of travel line (sometimes with an arrow at one end) to point toward your objective. The longer the base plate, the easier it is to get an accurate reading.

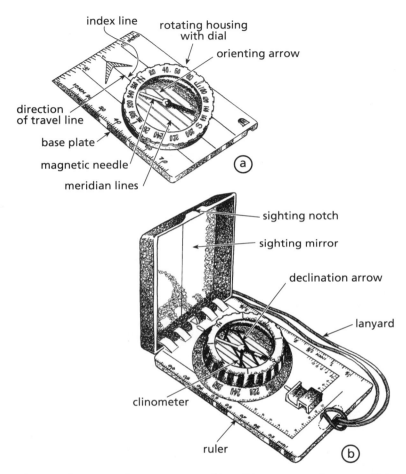

Figure 5. Features of compasses used in wilderness travel: a. essential features; b. useful optional features

The following are optional features (fig. 5b) available on some compasses:

- An adjustable declination arrow—an easy, dependable way to correct for magnetic declination; well worth the added cost.
- A sighting mirror—another way to improve accuracy.
- A ruler—calibrated in inches or millimeters. Use it for measuring short distances on a map.
- A clinometer—use it to measure the angle of a slope in the field.
- A magnifying glass—use it to help read closely spaced contour lines and other minute details on maps.

Some compasses have an adjustable declination arrow but no mirror. These cost a little more than the basic compass of figure 5a but considerably less than the mirrored compass of figure 5b. They offer a good compromise for someone who prefers the adjustable declination arrow but does not want to pay the added cost of the mirror.

Most compasses have a lanyard—a piece of string a foot or so long for attaching the compass to your belt, jacket, or pack. It is not a good idea to put the lanyard around your neck; this can be an unsafe practice, particularly when doing any technical climbing, difficult scrambling, or when climbing over and under fallen logs in a forest.

Small, round, cheap compasses without base plates are not accurate enough for wilderness travel, nor can you use them for working with a map (as will be explained below). For routefinding, the compass must be accurate to within 2 degrees. A larger error, say 5 degrees, can land a party a kilometer off target at the end of a 12-kilometer trip.

TYPES OF BASE PLATE COMPASSES

The base plate compasses listed here are the ones we know about as we go to press. By the time the book hits the streets, some of these may be discontinued, while still others may appear. But this listing should at least give you an idea of what types of compasses are available.

Minimal compasses: These meet all the basic requirements for wilderness travel, but do not have features such as mirrors or declination corrections: *Silva* Polaris 7 and Explorer 3; *Nexus* Nova 8NL, Star 7NL, and Explorer; *Suunto* A10, A30, A30L, A-1000, A-2100, and Geologist's compass.

With mirror but no declination adjustment: *Silva* Guide 26 and Trekker 20; *Suunto* Challenger MCA-D.

With declination adjustment but no mirror: *Suunto* Locator M2-D, Leader M3-D, Contender M5-DL, Smoke Killer M5SK, and GPS Plotter Compass; *Silva* Type 17; *Brunton* 8000, 8010, 8020, 8020GPS, and 9020.

Full-featured: These top-of-the-line compasses have declination adjustment, mirrors, and clinometers. Though more expensive than the compasses described above, these are best for wilderness navigation. *Silva* Ranger 15; *Suunto* Professional MC1-D and Global MC-1G; *Nexus* Ranger 15 and Ranger Pro 25; *Brunton* 8040, 8040 Elite, and Pro Line.

Unacceptable compasses: These have scales marked in 5 degree increments, or do not have rectangular, transparent base plates. Wrist and pin-on compasses are in this category.

If minimum cost is your primary concern, the compasses shown above as "minimal compasses" will work, though you will need to make a modification or adjustment to correct for magnetic declination. We will describe this later in the chapter.

If cost is not an important factor, any of the compasses listed as "full-featured" will give you all of the important features in a compass. We strongly recommend such a compass if you can afford it.

If you can afford a better compass than the "minimal" compasses but do not wish to spend enough to get a "full-featured" one, then we recommend getting a compass with a declination adjustment, but without a mirror or clinometer. Of all the optional features, the declination adjustment is the most useful. The reason for this will become apparent later in this chapter.

BEARINGS

A *bearing* is the direction from one place to another, measured in degrees of angle with respect to an accepted reference line. This reference is the line to true north.

The round dial of a compass is divided just as cartographers divide the earth, into 360 degrees. The direction in degrees to each of the cardinal directions, going clockwise around the dial starting from the top, is: north, 0 degrees (the same as 360 degrees); east, 90 degrees; south, 180 degrees; and west, 270 degrees.

The compass is used for two basic tasks regarding bearings:

1. The compass is used to *take bearings*. (You can also say that the compass is used to *measure bearings*.) To take a bearing means to measure the direction from one point to another, either on a map or in the field.
2. The compass is used to *plot bearings*. (You can also say that the compass is used to *follow bearings*.) To plot, or follow, a bearing means to set a certain bearing on the compass and then to plot out, or to follow, where that bearing points, on the map or in the field.

BEARINGS IN THE FIELD

All bearings in the field are based on where the needle points. For the sake of simplicity, we will first ignore the effects of magnetic declination, a subject that will be taken up in the next section. Let us imagine that we are in Wisconsin, where there is no declination.

Figure 6. Taking a compass bearing in the field in an area with no declination

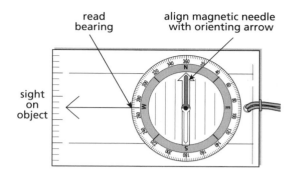

To take (measure) a bearing in the field: Hold the compass in front of you and point the direction of travel line at the object whose bearing you want to find. Then rotate the compass housing until the pointed end of the orienting arrow is aligned with the north-seeking (usually red) end of the magnetic needle. (This process is sometimes referred to as "boxing the needle" or "getting the dog in the doghouse.") Read the bearing at the index line (fig. 6).

If the compass has no sighting mirror, hold it at or near arm's length and at or near waist level, with your arm straight at about a 45 degree angle from your body. This is a compromise between sighting with the compass at eye level (sighting on your objective along the edge of the compass, but without being able to see the compass needle or orienting arrow) or holding it straight down (being able to see the compass needle and arrow without parallax but losing sight of the objective). With a sighting mirror, no such compromise is necessary. Fold the mirror back to about a 45 degree angle and hold the compass at eye level, with the sight pointing at the object. Observe the magnetic needle and the orienting arrow in the mirror as you rotate the housing to align the needle and the arrow. In either case, hold the compass level. Keep it away from metal objects, which can easily deflect the magnetic needle, giving you a false reading.

To follow (plot) a bearing in the field: Simply reverse the process you used to take a bearing. Rotate the compass housing until you have set the desired bearing at the index line, say 270 degrees (west). Then hold the compass level in front of you and turn your entire body (including your feet) until the north-seeking end of the magnetic needle is aligned with the pointed end of the orienting arrow (i.e., "box" the needle). The direction of travel line is now pointing in whatever direction you have set at the index line, in this case west.

MAGNETIC DECLINATION

A compass needle is attracted to *magnetic* north, while most maps are printed with true north—the direction to the geographic north pole—at the top. This difference between the direction to true north and the direction to magnetic north, measured in degrees, is called *magnetic declination*. You will need to make a simple compass adjustment or modification to correct for declination.

Magnetic declination varies from place to place and over time. Always use the latest topographic map for your area and find the amount and direction of declination on the map—near the lower left corner on USGS topographic maps. If the map is over ten years old, the declination may be somewhat out of date. The amount of declination changes over time up to 0.2 degrees per year in some places in the United States and even more in other parts of the world. This means that declination can change up to 2 degrees in a ten year period of time in the U.S. The map of the United States shown in figure 7 will give you a fairly good idea of declination in your area. The map is for 1999 and will be valid until about 2004.

In figure 7, you can see that the line of zero declination runs through Wisconsin, Illinois, western Tennessee, and Mississippi. Along this line, the magnetic needle points in the same direction as the geographic north pole (true north), so no correction for declination is necessary. But in areas west of this line, the magnetic needle points somewhere to the east (to the right) of true north, so these areas are said to have *east declination*. It works just the opposite on the other side of the line of zero declination, such as on the East Coast. Here, the magnetic needle points somewhere to the west (left) of true north, so these areas are said to have *west declination*.

Consider a wilderness traveler in the state of Nevada, with a declination of 15 degrees east. The true bearing is a measurement of the angle between the line to true north and the line to the objective, as shown in figure 7. The magnetic needle, however, is pulled toward magnetic north, not true north. So instead it measures the angle between the line to magnetic north and the line to the objective. This "magnetic bearing" is 15 degrees less than the true bearing. To get the true bearing, you could *add* 15 degrees to the magnetic bearing.

As in Nevada, travelers in all areas west of the zero declination line could add the declination to the magnetic bearing to get a true bearing. In western Colorado, for example, about 12 degrees would be added. In the central part of the state of Washington, it is about 19 degrees.

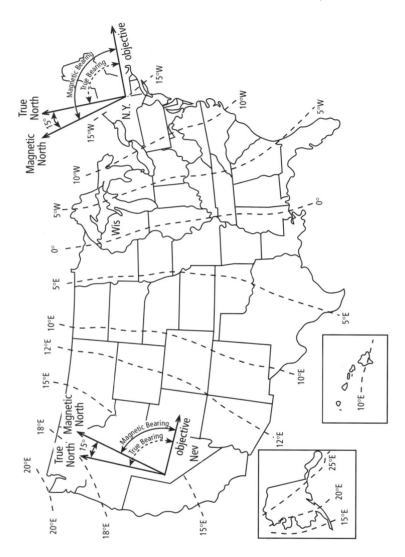

Figure 7. Magnetic declination in the United States in 1999

East of the zero declination line, the declination can be *subtracted* from the magnetic bearing to get the true bearing. In eastern New York, for example, the magnetic bearing is about 15 degrees greater than the true bearing. To get a true bearing, the traveler in New York could subtract the declination of 15 degrees from the magnetic bearing.

This is all very simple in theory but can be confusing in practice, and the wilderness is no place for mental arithmetic that can potentially have serious consequences. A more practical way to handle the minor complication of declination is to pay somewhat more for your compass and get one with an adjustable *declination arrow* instead of a fixed orienting arrow. You can easily set the declination arrow for any declination by following the instructions supplied with the compass—usually by inserting a tiny screwdriver (often attached to the lanyard) into a small slot and turning it until the declination arrow points at the correct value. Then the bearing that you read at the index line will automatically be the true bearing, and concern about a declination error is one worry you can leave at home. Compasses with adjustable declination arrows are sometimes called "set and forget" compasses.

On compasses without adjustable declination arrows, you can get the same effect by sticking a thin strip of tape to the bottom of the rotating housing to serve as a customized declination arrow. Trim the tape to a point, and apply it to the bottom of the compass for the area where you will be traveling, as shown in figure 8.

In Nevada, your taped declination arrow must point at 15 degrees east (clockwise) from the 360 degree point (marked N for north) on the rotating dial (fig. 8a). In New York, the declination arrow must point at 15 degrees west (counterclockwise) from the 360 degree mark (fig. 8b), or 345 degrees. In the central part of the state of Washington, the declination arrow must point at 19 degrees east (clockwise) from 360 degrees.

If you travel in an area where the declination is different, you will have to change the declination correction. If you have a compass with an adjustable declination arrow, a minor screwdriver adjustment will allow you to set the compass for the new declination. If you have a taped declination arrow, you will have to peel the tape off and put a new one on, to correct for the new declination.

To take a bearing in the field, follow exactly the same procedure used in the earlier examples for Wisconsin. The only difference is that, from now on, you will align the magnetic needle with the *declination arrow* instead of with the orienting arrow. Always remember to align the *north-seeking (usually red) end* of the magnetic needle with the *pointed end* of the declination arrow to "box" the needle.

From here on in this book, we will assume that you are using a compass with a declination arrow—either an adjustable arrow or a

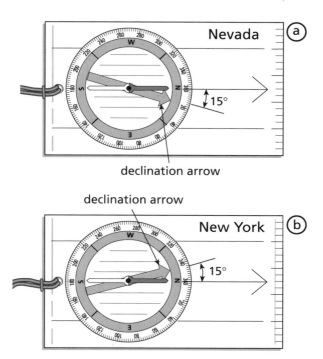

Figure 8. Compass declination arrow placement: a. for area west of the zero declination line; b. for area east of the zero declination line

taped arrow that you have added. For all bearings in the field, you will align the needle with this declination arrow. All compass bearings used from this point on are true bearings. We will not refer to magnetic bearings again, since we always automatically convert all bearings to true ones.

WHERE TO GET DECLINATION INFORMATION

If the information in figure 7 is not adequate for your purposes, you can buy a copy of a map called the *Magnetic Field of the U.S. Declination Chart* from the USGS, P.O. Box 25286, Denver, CO 80225. You can call the USGS at 1-800-435-7627 to order it.

There are also some Web sites on the Internet where declination information is available. One is the *Canadian Geomagnetic Reference Field (CGRF)*, whose site can be found at the following address: http://www.geolab.nrcan.gc.ca/geomag/e_cgrf.html.

This will give you present time declination for anywhere in the northern hemisphere. Just tell it what set of latitude and longitude coordinates you want, found at any corner of your topographic map. The CGRF can also give you declination for several years in the past and in the future.

In most parts of the world, you can buy topographic maps with declination information. If you go somewhere where you cannot find the declination, you can get a fairly close estimate of it from figure 9.

DIP

The magnetic needle of the compass is not only affected by the horizontal direction of the earth's magnetic field, but also by its vertical pull. The closer you get to the magnetic north pole, the more the north-seeking end of the needle tends to point *downward*. At the magnetic equator, the needle will be level, while at the south magnetic pole the north-seeking end of the needle tries to point in an *upward* direction. This phenomenon is referred to as the compass *dip*. To compensate for this effect, most compass manufacturers purposely introduce a slight imbalance to the magnetic needles of their compasses, so that their dip is negligible for the geographic area where they will be used. They divide the earth into dip zones, and compasses sold in each zone are compensated for use in that zone.

If you buy a compass in one dip zone and try to use it in another, the compass may not work well because of the difference in dip. For example, if you buy a compass in North America or Europe and then try to use it in Kenya, New Zealand, or some other faraway place, the difference in dip may be enough to introduce errors in your compass readings or even make the compass impossible to use. For this reason, if you bring your compass to a faraway place, you should first try it out in an urban area as soon as you arrive, to make sure it works properly *before* heading out into the wilderness. If it is adversely affected by dip, you may have to buy a new compass in the general area where you will be traveling. Most compasses sold anywhere in the world are compensated for dip in that particular zone.

Another way of ensuring that you will not have this problem is to buy a compass ahead of time which is properly compensated for dip in the area you will be visiting. Some retail stores and mail-order companies have or can order compasses compensated for whatever zone you will be visiting. Doing this in advance of your visit will ensure that you will not have a problem with compass dip during your travels.

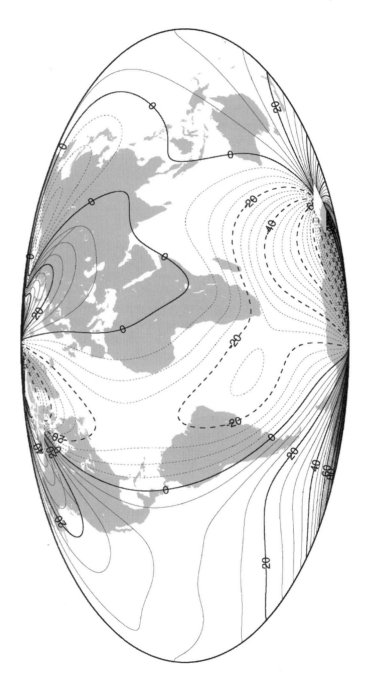

Figure 9. World magnetic declination for 1999: Lines of constant declination are at 5-degree intervals. Solid lines indicate east declination; dashed lines indicate west declination. Source: IAGA Working Group V-8 and AGSO

BACK BEARINGS

A *back bearing* is the opposite direction of a bearing. This is also sometimes referred to as a *reciprocal* bearing. Back bearings are often useful when you are trying to follow a certain bearing, and you want to check to see if you are still on the bearing line by taking a *back bearing* on your starting point. For example, if you have a bearing of 90 degrees, then the back bearing is 270 degrees. If your bearing is less than 180 degrees, then you can find the back bearing by adding 180 degrees. If your bearing is greater than 180 degrees, then you can find the back bearing by subtracting 180 degrees from the original bearing.

We previously mentioned that we do not recommend mental arithmetic in the wilderness, since it is too easy to make mistakes. There are two other ways of dealing with back bearings, without using mental arithmetic. One way is to set your bearing at the index line of your compass, and then to look at the point on the compass dial *opposite* the index line. The number on the dial at this point is the back bearing. Another way of working with a back bearing is to set the bearing at the index line, and get the direction of travel line to point at the back bearing by aligning the *south-seeking end* (the white or black end) of the magnetic needle with the pointed end of the declination arrow. We will describe the use of back bearings in some of the following chapters.

BEARINGS ON THE MAP

You can use your compass as a protractor, both to measure and to plot bearings on a map. Magnetic north and magnetic declination have nothing to do with these operations. Therefore, ignore the magnetic needle when measuring or plotting bearings on a map. (The only time you need to use the magnetic needle when working with the map is whenever you choose to orient the map to true north, which we will explain in the next chapter. But there is no need to orient the map to measure or plot bearings.)

To measure a bearing on a map: Place the compass on the map with one long edge of the base plate running between the two points of interest. To measure the bearing from point *A* to point *B*, see that the direction of travel line is pointing in the direction *from A to B.* Then turn the rotating housing until its set of meridian lines is parallel to the north-south lines of the map. Be sure that the *N* on the compass dial is toward the top of the map and that the *S* is toward the bottom. (If you put the *N* toward the bottom of the map, with the *S* toward the top, your reading will be 180 degrees off.) For the utmost in accuracy, slide the compass along the bearing line so that one of its meridian lines is exactly on top of one of the north-south lines on the map. Now read the number that is at the index line. This is the bearing from point *A* to point *B*.

Suppose you are at the summit of Panic Peak, and you want to know which of the many peaks around you is Deception Dome. Your map shows both peaks (fig. 10), so you can measure the bearing from point *A*, Panic Peak, to point *B*, Deception Dome. The result, as read at the index line, is 35 degrees. (In this figure, we have purposely omitted the magnetic needle for the sake of clarity.) You can then hold the compass out in front of you and turn your entire body until you "box" the needle. The direction of travel line will then point toward Deception Dome and you can identify it.

To plot a bearing on the map: In this case you are starting with a known bearing. And where does that bearing come from? From an actual landscape compass reading. Let us take a hypothetical example: Your friend returns from a backpacking trip, remorseful for having left a camera somewhere along the trail. While at a rest

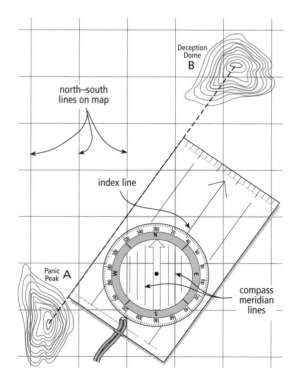

Figure 10.
Measuring a
bearing on
a map with the
compass as a
protractor
(magnetic
needle omitted
for clarity)

north–south
lines on map

Deception
Dome
B

index line

Panic
Peak **A**

compass
meridian
lines

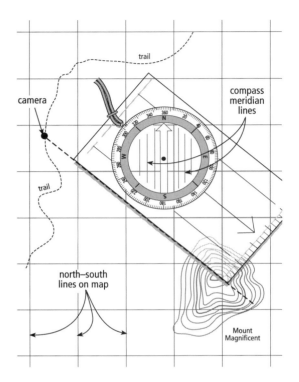

Figure 11. Plotting a bearing on a map with the compass as a protractor (magnetic needle omitted for clarity)

stop, your friend had taken a bearing on Mount Magnificent and found it to be 130 degrees. That is all you need to know. You are heading into that same area next week, so get out the Magnificent quadrangle, and here is what you do:

First set the bearing of 130 degrees at the compass index line. Place the compass on the map, one long edge of the base plate touching the summit of Mount Magnificent (fig. 11). Rotate the entire compass (not just the housing) until the meridian lines in the compass housing are parallel with the map's north-south lines, and make sure that the edge of the base plate is still touching the summit. Again, be sure that the N on the compass dial is toward the top of the map. Draw a line along the edge of the base plate. Where this line crosses the trail is where your friend's camera is (or was).

When measuring or plotting bearings on a map, the map does not need to be in a horizontal position, such as lying down on the snow or dirt, on a stump, or in the mud. Instead, it can be vertical or in any other position. Its orientation doesn't matter, since you are just using the compass as a protractor. In the forest, you can place the compass up against a tree to do the map and compass work. On a snowfield or glacier, with no trees, you can instead ask another member of the party to stand still while you steady the map against the person's back. Or you can sit down on your pack, and do the map work with the map in your lap or on your knee with your leg crossed.

PRACTICING WITH THE COMPASS

Before you count on your compass skills in the wilderness, test them in the city. The best place to practice is at a place where you already know all the answers, like a street intersection where the roads run north-south and east-west.

Take a bearing in a direction you know to be east. When you have pointed the direction of travel line at something that you know is east of you, such as along the edge of the street or sidewalk, and have "boxed" the needle, the number at the index line should be very close to 90 degrees. Repeat for the other cardinal directions: south, west, and north. Then try all four again to see how repeatable the bearings are. Try to refine your technique to improve your accuracy. You may have to hold the compass higher or lower, or perhaps close one eye. Find out what amount of accuracy you can get.

Then try the reverse process. Pretend you do not know which way is west. Set 270 degrees (west) at the index line and hold the compass out in front of you as you turn your entire body (including your feet) until the needle is "boxed." The direction of travel line should now point west. Does it? Repeat for the other three cardinal directions. This set of exercises will help you to develop skill and self-confidence at compass reading and is also a way to check the accuracy of your compass. And if you make a mistake or two, well, no harm done.

You can practice measuring and plotting bearings on a map using the examples shown in figures 10 and 11. These figures are drawn with the correct angular proportions, so you can place your compass on the page and you should get the same answers we get. For additional practice, more map and compass problems and answers are given in the appendix of this book.

If you ever doubt the accuracy of your compass—perhaps because it has developed a small bubble or has given you a questionable reading in the field—take the compass out to the street intersection again to test it. If the bearings you read are more than a few degrees away from the correct ones, consider replacing your compass.

Look for places to practice in the wilderness. A good place is any known location (such as a summit or a lakeshore) from which you can see identifiable landmarks. Take bearings on some of these and plot them on the map to see how close the result is to your actual location.

TIPS ON COMPASS USE

There is a big difference between using a compass for working with a map and using a compass for field work. In the field, you must use the magnetic needle to "box" the needle by aligning the *pointed end* of the declination arrow with the *red end* of the magnetic needle. When measuring and plotting bearings on a map, however, you should ignore the compass needle. Just align the meridian lines in the compass housing with the north-south lines on the map, with the N of the compass dial toward north on the map. In both cases, the direction of travel line must point *from* you *to* your objective.

You may have heard that nearby metal can mess up a compass. This is true. Ferrous objects such as iron and steel will deflect the magnetic needle and give false readings. Keep the compass away from belt buckles, ice axes, and other metal objects. If a compass reading does not make sense, see if nearby metal is sabotaging your bearing.

Keep your wits about you when pointing the direction of travel line and the declination arrow. If you point either of them backward—an easy thing to do—the reading will be 180 degrees off. If the bearing is north, the compass will say it is south. Remember that the north-seeking (usually red) end of the magnetic needle must be aligned with the pointed end of the declination arrow and that the direction of travel line must point *from* you *to* your objective.

Whenever you measure or plot bearings on a map, it is a good idea to first *guess* at the answer. Then if the bearing you carefully measure or plot is nowhere near your original guess, you may have made one of those 180 degree errors. For example, suppose you want to measure a bearing on a map, and this bearing is somewhere between northeast (45 degrees) and east (90 degrees). You might guess that it is 60 or 80 degrees or so. Then you measure the bearing as accurately as possible using your compass. You line up one of the compass meridian lines exactly on top of one of the map's north-south lines, getting the bearing accurate to the nearest degree, and the number you read at your index line is 247 degrees. Does this agree with your original guess? *No!* You must have made a 180 degree mistake, and the correct answer is 67 degrees.

When taking and following bearings in the field, you can also begin by making an intelligent guess at the result, then using the compass to get the exact answer. Before blindly following the compass, you can then ask yourself if the result from the compass agrees with your rough guess. If not, perhaps you have made one of those 180-degree errors.

If in doubt, trust your compass. The compass, correctly used, is almost always right, while your contrary judgment may be clouded by fatigue, confusion, or hurry. If you get a nonsensical reading, check to see if perhaps you are making one of those 180-degree errors. If not, and if no metal is in sight, verify the reading with other members of the party, using different compasses. If they get the same answer, trust your compass over hunches, blind guesses, and intuition.

USE OF THE CLINOMETER

If you have a compass with a clinometer, you can use it to measure angles of slope. First, set either 90 degrees or 270 degrees at the index line of the compass. Then hold the compass with its long edge level, so that the clinometer needle points down toward the numbered scale (which may be the same scale used for declination adjustment). With the direction of travel line level, the clinometer should read zero. Tilting the compass up or down will cause the clinometer needle to point to the number of degrees upward or downward.

There are two ways to use the clinometer. The first is to measure the angle to a distant object. For example, suppose you are at the summit of some peak, and you see another peak of nearly the same elevation, and you wonder if you are on the higher of the two summits. Hold the compass with its long edge pointing toward the other peak, as you sight along the long edge of the base plate at it. Steady the compass on a rock or other stable object if possible. Tap the compass lightly to overcome any friction in the mechanism, and ask a companion to look at the clinometer needle to see if it indicates an upward or a downward angle toward the other peak. If it indicates an upward angle, then the other peak is higher than you are. Sorry.

The clinometer can also be used to find the angle of the slope. In chapter 1, we explained how to determine the angle of slope from a map. The clinometer, however, can tell you the actual angle of the slope on which you are standing. Just set 90 degrees or 270 degrees at the index line, and lay the long edge of the compass on the slope. Then read the angle of slope on the clinometer scale. Due to variations in the slope over small distances, it is best to place an ice ax, ski pole, or other long object along the slope, and place the long edge of the compass along this object to get a better idea of the average slope. The presence of metal, such as an ice ax or ski pole shaft, will affect the magnetic needle, but not the clinometer needle, which works with gravity.

OTHER TYPES OF COMPASSES

Base plate compasses sold under the names of *Silva, Suunto,* and *Nexus* are similar to the ones shown in figure 5, and the methods of using these compasses are as described above. Several *Brunton* base plate compasses are also available. These work slightly differently from the others, but they are also acceptable for use in wilderness navigation.

Most *Brunton* compasses have adjustable declination arrows, but there is no screwdriver adjustment as there is with other compasses. Instead, the *Brunton* has a round capsule within the rotating housing. To adjust for declination, you simply lightly squeeze this capsule between the thumb and forefinger of one hand while you grasp the rotating housing with your other hand. Then you can turn the capsule to get the declination arrow to point to the correct number of degrees (e.g., 15 degrees in Nevada, or 345 degrees in New York). Then the compass is used in the same way as described above for other compasses. The needle is "boxed" by aligning the pointed end of the declination arrow with the red end of the magnetic needle.

The procedure for measuring and plotting bearings on maps is also slightly different for *Brunton* compasses, since they either have no meridian lines in the rotating housing, or have meridian lines which turn along with the declination arrow, and are therefore not aligned with north and south on the compass dial. But most such compasses have partial meridian lines, aligned with north and south on the dial, on the outer ring of the rotating housing. To measure or plot bearings on a map, follow the procedures described above for other compasses, except that you should align the partial meridian lines on the outside ring with the north-south lines on the map. As with the other compasses, always make sure that the N on the rotating compass dial is aligned towards north (usually the top) of the map.

Some base plate compasses have rotating housings which are

marked from zero to 90 degrees and back to zero, and then to 90 degrees and back to zero again. These are called *quadrant* types, and some people prefer them. We do not recommend these for wilderness navigation, since using them requires the use of mental arithmetic, and you know what we think of *that*. Bearings taken with a quadrant compass are often expressed as the number of degrees east or west of north or south, such as S 20° E, which means 20 degrees east of south, or 180 degrees minus 20 degrees equals 160 degrees.

We have recommended that you get a *base plate* compass, and we wrote all the examples of taking, following, measuring, and plotting bearings on the assumption that you are using a base plate compass. There are, however, other types of compasses, most notably optical sighting compasses, such as the *Plastimo* Iris 50, the *Accusight*, the *Vion* Mini 2000, the *Suunto* KB-14/360, KB-20, and KB-77, the *Brunton* Sight Master, the *Lensatic* and *Prismatic* compasses, and others. There are even battery-operated digital compasses such as the *Autohelm* digital hand bearing compass. These are generally more accurate and more precise than most base plate compasses and are useful if the accuracy you need is not possible with a base plate compass. Most of these are not available with declination adjustments, so you need to add or subtract declination. Also, most of these are not base plate compasses, so with these you also need to bring along a protractor or a base plate compass to measure and plot bearings.

One particularly interesting optical sighting compass is the *Silva* Surveyor Type 54, which is an optical sighting *base plate* compass which also works in a non-optical sighting mode. You can correct it for declination by using a taped declination arrow, as described earlier in this chapter, but this only works for the non-optical mode. To take advantage of the added accuracy provided by the optical mode, you have to add or subtract declination. But since it is a base plate compass, you can use it for measuring and plotting bearings on a map, unlike most other optical sighting compasses.

Base plate compasses can be found at most outdoor recreation stores, while nautical supply stores usually carry optical sighting compasses. In addition, several mail-order companies sell compasses, altimeters, GPS receivers, and other equipment of interest to the wilderness traveler. Two of these are the Ben Meadows Company (1-800-241-6401) and Forestry Suppliers, Inc. (1-800-647-5368).

THE MAP AND COMPASS: A CHECKLIST

Do you have the hang of it? There are four essential compass operations that you must learn: taking and following bearings in the field, and measuring and plotting bearings on the map. Let us summarize these one last time. Check off each operation as you do it.

☐ To Take a Bearing in the Field

1. Hold compass level, in front of you, and point direction of travel line at desired object.
2. Rotate compass housing to align pointed end of declination arrow with red end of magnetic needle. ("Box" the needle.)
3. Read bearing at index line.

☐ To Follow a Bearing in the Field

1. Set desired bearing at index line.
2. Hold compass level, in front of you, and turn your entire body, including your feet, until red end of magnetic needle is aligned with pointed end of declination arrow. ("Box" the needle.)
3. Travel in the direction shown by the direction of travel line.

☐ To Measure a Bearing on a Map (see figure 10)

1. Place compass on map, with one long edge of base plate joining two points of interest. Direction of travel line points to objective.
2. Rotate housing to align compass meridian lines with north-south lines on map, with N on compass toward top of map.
3. Read bearing at index line.

☐ To Plot a Bearing on a Map (see figure 11)

1. Set desired bearing at index line.
2. Place compass on map, with one long edge of base plate on feature from which you wish to plot bearing.
3. Turn entire compass to align its meridian lines with map's north-south lines, with N on compass toward top of map. The edge of the base plate is now the bearing line.

Whenever you perform any of these operations, first guess at the answer, then perform the operation as accurately as you can. Then compare your answer to your original guess to ensure that you are not making a 180-degree error.

AND FOR THE LAST TIME:

- When taking and following bearings in the field, always align the pointed end of the declination arrow with the north-seeking (usually red) end of the magnetic needle. ("Box" the needle.)
- Never use the magnetic needle or the declination arrow when measuring or plotting bearings on the map. Just make sure that the N on the compass dial is toward north on the map, not south, as a check to ensure that the compass meridian lines are not upside-down.

Once you master these four essential operations with the compass, you will have all the knowledge you need for map-and-compass orientation, navigation, and routefinding. Everything in the following chapters of this book is based on these four operations. If you thoroughly understand how to do these four things, you can proceed through the rest of the book with confidence, and you will easily understand everything that we explain.

If you are unsure of any of these four operations, we suggest that you stop now and reread this chapter. Study it carefully. Do the simple street-corner compass exercises we described for taking and following bearings. Measure and plot the bearings shown in figure 10 and figure 11. Additional practice problems are given in the appendix. You must thoroughly understand each of these four operations before proceeding with the rest of this book.

Once you thoroughly understand maps and the four basic operations of the compass, you are ready for orientation with map and compass.

ORIENTATION WITH MAP AND COMPASS

Figuring out exactly where you are is usually a relatively simple affair, done by just looking around and comparing what you see with what is on a map. Sometimes this is not accurate enough, or there is just nothing much nearby to identify on the map. The usual solution then is to get out the compass and to try for bearings on some landscape features. This is orientation by instrument. But before resorting to orientation by instrument, first study the map carefully to see if there are any topographic features—even subtle ones—that you can associate with the landscape around you. If you have been carefully observing your map and comparing it with the landscape, as we suggested in chapter 1, you should have a fairly good idea of where you are. Orientation by instrument should be reserved for situations in which nothing else works, for compass practice, or for verifying your location after using other methods.

The goal of orientation is to determine that precise point on the surface of the earth where you now stand. You can represent your position by a mere dot on the map. This is known as *point position*. There are two lower levels of orientation. One is called *line position*: you know you are along a certain line on a map—such as a river, a trail, a ridge, a compass bearing, or a contour line—but not where you are along the line. The lowest level of orientation is *area position*: you know the general area you are in, but that is all. The primary objective of orientation is to find out your exact point position.

POINT POSITION

With point position known, you know exactly where you are, and you can use that knowledge to identify, on the map, any major

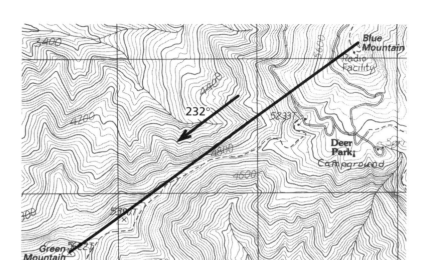

Figure 12. Example of point position *(Illustration by J. Shontz)*

feature that you can see in the landscape. You can also identify in the landscape any major visible feature that is shown on the map.

For example, suppose you have hiked to the summit of Blue Mountain. You know your point position: the top of Blue Mountain. You see an unknown peak and want to know what it is. You take a compass bearing on it and get 232 degrees. You plot 232 degrees from Blue Mountain on your map, and the plotted line passes through Green Mountain (fig. 12). The unknown peak is Green Mountain.

However, if you start by wanting to find which of the many peaks around you is Green Mountain, you must do the map work first. You measure the bearing on the map from where you are, Blue Mountain, to Green Mountain, and get 232 degrees. Keeping the 232 degrees at the index line, the entire compass is turned until the needle is "boxed." The direction of travel line then points toward Green Mountain.

LINE POSITION

With line position known, the goal is to determine point position. If you know that you are on a trail, ridge, or some other easily identifiable line, you need only one more trustworthy piece of information to get your point position. For example, suppose a party of scramblers is on Unsavory Ridge, but they do not know exactly where they are on the ridge. In the distance is Mount Majestic. A bearing on it indicates 220 degrees. They plot 220 degrees from Mount Majestic on the map, and run this line back toward Unsavory Ridge (fig. 13). Where it intersects the ridge is where the scramblers are.

Figure 13. Orientation, line position known (magnetic needle omitted for clarity)

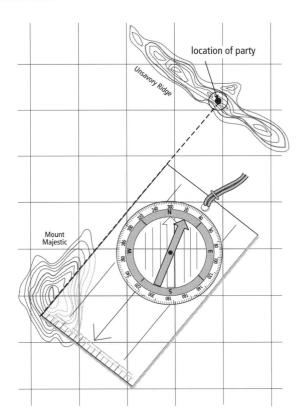

location of party

Unsavory Ridge

Mount Majestic

AREA POSITION

Some snowshoers know their area position: they are in the general area of Fantastic Crags. They want to determine line position and then, from that, point position. To move from knowing area position to knowing point position, they need two trustworthy pieces of information (fig. 14).

They may be able to use bearings on two visible features. They take a bearing on Fantastic Peak and get a reading of 40 degrees. They plot a line on the map, along the base plate and through

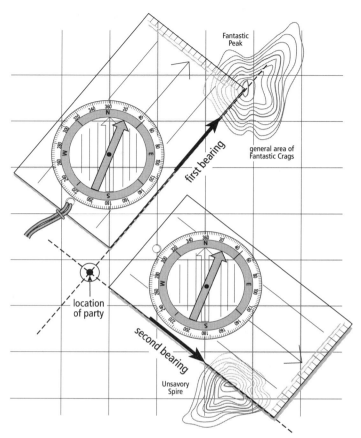

Figure 14. Orientation, area position known (magnetic needle omitted for clarity)

Fantastic Peak, at 40 degrees. They know they must be somewhere on that bearing line, so they now have line position. They can also see Unsavory Spire. A bearing on the spire shows 130 degrees. They plot this line on the map, through Unsavory Spire, and draw a line along the base plate. The two bearing lines intersect, and that is where they are.

Or approximately so. Whenever you take a bearing in the field or plot a bearing on a map, it is inevitable that minor errors will creep in to create larger errors in the estimate of your position. It is very easy to make an error of 3 degrees in taking a bearing, and another 2 degrees in plotting that bearing, unless you are extremely careful. For every 5 degrees of error, your position will be in error

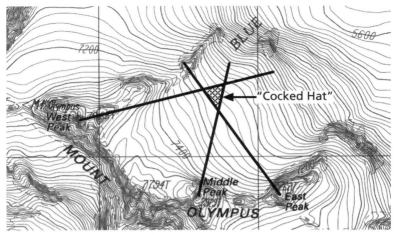

Figure 15. Plotting three bearings results in a "cocked hat" position. *(Illustration by J. Shontz)*

by about 90 meters in every km, or about 460 feet in every mile. If you take and plot a bearing on a landmark three miles away, and make a 5 degree error, the plotted line might be about 1400 feet away from the correct position. Therefore, be sure that your conclusions agree with common sense. If you take and plot bearings from two peaks and find that the two lines intersect in the middle of a river, but you are standing on a high point of land, something is wrong. Try again. Try to take a more accurate bearing, and plot it more carefully. If bearing lines intersect at a map location with no similarity to the terrain, you may have errors in your bearings. Or there might be some magnetic anomaly in the rocks, or you might have an inaccurate map. And who knows? Maybe those peaks are not really the peaks you think they are. Make sure that the two bearings are not from approximately the same direction, since this can compound any error. The closer an angle of intersection is to 90 degrees, the more accurate the point position will be.

The technique of taking and plotting bearings from landmarks is more accurate if you can see *three* landmarks and plot three bearings. The result will be a small triangle (called a "cocked hat," see fig. 15). Your position is within this triangle, or at least close to it.

ORIENTING A MAP

During a trip it sometimes helps to hold the map so that north on the map is pointed in the actual direction of true north. This is

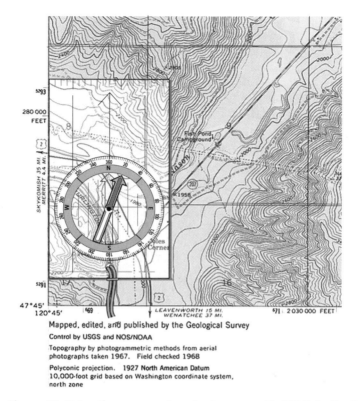

Figure 16. Using the compass to orient a map with 20° E declination

known as orienting the map, a good way to obtain a better feel of the relationship between the map and the countryside.

One way to orient a map is *by inspection*: simply look at the terrain and compare it with the map. Then hold the map level and turn it until the map is lined up with the terrain.

Often, this technique will not work because you cannot see any identifiable features around you. In this case, you can orient your map using your compass. Set 360 degrees (north) at the index line of the compass and place your compass on the map. Put one long edge of the base plate along the left edge of the map as shown in figure 16. Then turn the map and compass together until the needle is "boxed." The map is now oriented to the scene around you. (Map orientation can give you a general feel for the area but cannot replace the precise methods of orientation that we covered in the preceding paragraphs.)

DIRECTION AND BEARING OF THE SLOPE

You can often help to find your position by using the *direction of the slope,* which was first described in chapter 1. For example, suppose you are hiking along the trail near Maiden Peak and want to find your point position. You take a bearing on Maiden Peak and get 242 degrees, as shown in figure 17. You plot this bearing and find that it crosses the trail in two places, *A* and *B*. Where are you? Points *A* and *B* are both on a ridge, but at point *A* the slope falls off to the east and the west, while at point *B* it falls off to the north and the south. Suppose you take your compass and point it in the direction of the slope. You find that the actual slope falls off to the north and south. That tells you that you are at point *B*, not point *A*.

Sometimes the situation is a little more subtle, so we need more precision with this approach. In this case, we refer to the *bearing of the slope* rather than merely its general direction. Imagine that another party is also on the Maiden Peak trail and wants to find its position. Some party members take a bearing on Maiden Peak and get 42 degrees. They plot this line, as shown in figure 17, and they

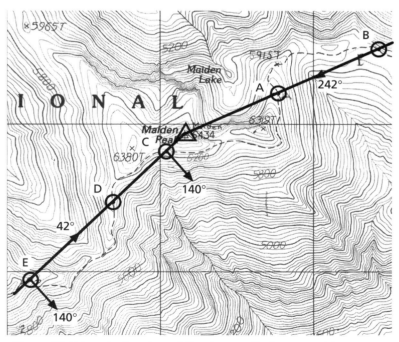

Figure 17. Using the bearing of the slope to find your position
(Illustration by J. Shontz)

see that the bearing line crosses the trail in *three* places. Where are they, point C, D, or E? A quick compass bearing shows that the slope falls off roughly to the southeast, so point D is ruled out, since at that point the map clearly shows the slope to fall off to the east and west. That narrows it down to either point C or point E. A party member faces downhill and takes a more careful bearing in the direction of the fall line. Suppose the bearing is 140 degrees. One long edge of the compass is then placed on the map at point C, and the entire compass is rotated until the meridian lines in the compass housing are parallel with the north-south lines on the map, with the N on the compass dial toward the top of the map. The edge of the base plate should then point in a direction perpendicular to the contour lines at point C. However, you can see that the bearing of 140 degrees is *not* perpendicular to the contour lines at point C. So instead the same process can be repeated for point E. This time, the bearing line is nearly perpendicular to the contour lines, at least for the first 200 feet down from point E. From this, the party concludes that it is at point E.

A REMINDER

At the beginning of this chapter we said that orientation by instrument should be reserved for those situations in which nothing else works. We wish to remind you that the best method of orientation is to use your map and your continual observations of topography to keep track of where you are. Presumably, at the beginning of your trek you know where you are and can identify that position on the map. If you then follow your progress on the map, noting each topographic or other feature that you pass, then at any time you should know your position with a great amount of certainty. It is essential to know the technical methods of map and compass orientation, but there is still no substitute for keeping track of your position using the map. If you faithfully do this, it is unlikely that you will ever get lost.

LOST!

The primary focus of this entire book is to give you the skills and knowledge needed to avoid getting lost in the first place. Later in this chapter we will give you some suggestions concerning what to do if you ever *do* get lost. But if you have carefully read and absorbed the preceding three chapters, carry a compass and a topographic map of the area, and have adequately practiced map reading, compass use, and orientation, you should always be able to know where you are. If so, you are not lost, and this entire subject may only be of academic interest to you. In addition to the information provided in the first three chapters, the information given below may go a long way towards preventing you from ever getting lost.

HOW TO AVOID GETTING LOST

BEFORE THE TRIP

Most wilderness orientation, navigation, and routefinding is done by simply looking at your surroundings and comparing them with the map. This process is often aided by making some navigational preparations before the trip, like identifying *handrails*, *base lines*, and possible routefinding problems.

A *handrail* is a linear feature on the map that you can follow, or it may be a feature that parallels the direction in which you are heading. The handrail should be within frequent sight of the route, so it can serve as an aid in navigation. Features that you can use from time to time as handrails during a trip include roads, trails, powerlines, railroad tracks, fences, borders of fields and meadows, valleys, streams, cliff bands, ridges, lakeshores, and the edges of marshes.

Another map technique can help in finding the way home if you have gotten off track. This is the use of a *base line*: a long, unmistakable line that always lies in the same direction from you, no matter where you are during the trip. Pick out a base line on the map during trip planning. It does not have to be something you can see during the trip. You just have to know that it is there, in a consistent direction from you. A base line (sometimes called a *catch line*) can be a road, a good, obvious trail, the shore of a large lake, a river, a powerline, or any other feature that is at least as long as your trip area. If the shore of a distant lake always lies west of the area you will be in, you can be sure that heading west at any time will eventually get you to this identifiable landmark. Heading toward this base line may not be the fastest way to travel back home from your destination, but it may save you from being truly lost.

Before the trip, it is wise to prepare a *route plan* and to trace out the entire trip on a topographic map. Identify handrails, base lines, and other features that you will be following on the way to your objective. Part of this plan is to recognize potential routefinding problems. For example, if the route traverses a large, featureless area, you may need route-marking materials, particularly if the weather outlook is marginal. Be sure to consider carrying such materials if your route plan indicates a possible need for them. Make a note of any "escape routes" that can be used in case of sudden bad weather or other setbacks. If off-trail travel is involved, you can measure compass bearings at home before the trip and write them down in a notebook or note them on the map. It is certainly possible to measure map bearings at any point in the trip, but it is easier at home on your kitchen table and might save you time in an emergency. Your route plan should be written down, and you should discuss this plan with other members of the party, so that the party is not solely depending on one person for all route decisions.

Another thing you should do before the trip is to tell a responsible person where you are going, what route you are taking, and when you plan on returning. This will not prevent you from getting lost. But if you do run into trouble, the authorities will know to look for you, and where to look. This one bit of preparation could save your life.

Always make sure that every member of the party will be carrying adequate food, clothing, and other supplies. In the event of any emergency, each person should have enough food and clothing to survive several days, if necessary, while waiting for searchers or rescue personnel to arrive. Every party member should carry a map of the area and a compass, in case someone gets separated from the group.

DURING THE TRIP

Get off on the right foot by making sure that everyone understands the route and the route plan. Gather the party around a map and take time to discuss the route and to make contingency plans in case the party gets separated. Point out on the map where you are, and associate your surroundings with the piece of paper in front of you. This is a good time for everyone to make a mental note of the main features the party will see during the trip, such as forests, streams, ridges, valleys, mountain peaks, and trails.

Along the way, everyone needs to keep associating the terrain with the map. Ignorance of the territory is definitely not bliss for any daydreaming person who gets separated from the party. Whenever a new landmark appears, connect it with the map. At every chance—at a pass, in a clearing, or through a break in the clouds—update your fix on the group's exact position. Keeping track of your progress this way makes it easy to plan each succeeding leg of the trip. It may also turn you into an expert map reader because you will quickly learn what a specific valley or ridge looks like compared with its representation on the map.

Use handrails wherever possible. When the inevitable moment comes when you must leave the security of your handrail, make a mental note of the fact that you are leaving it, and ask yourself what you will be following instead: some topographic feature, a contour line, a compass bearing, or anything else you can count on. You should not merely press onward with no clear idea of where you are headed or how to get back.

Keep the party together, except perhaps on well-traveled, obvious trails. Even then, do not let the group get too spread out, and agree ahead of time on places to stop and wait for everyone to catch up. If the group includes children or inexperienced persons, they should be kept in sight at all times. Assign a responsible, experienced person to be the rear guard, or "sweep," to ensure that no straggler will get left behind or lost.

Look Ahead to the Return Trip

The route always looks amazingly different on the way back. Avoid surprises and confusion by glancing back over your shoulder often on the way in to see what the route should look like on the return. If you cannot keep track of it all, jot down times, elevations, landmarks, and so on in a small notebook. A few cryptic words, such as "7600, hit ridge," can save you a lot of grief on the return. It will remind you that when the party has dropped to 7600 feet, it is time to leave the ridge and start down the slope to your starting point.

Think

Your brain is your most important navigational tool, a fact often overlooked amid our reliance on compasses, altimeters, and GPS receivers. As the party heads toward its destination, keep asking yourself questions: How will we recognize this important spot on our return? What would we do if the trip leader became unconscious? (Are we all placing total reliance on one person?) Could I get back myself if I had to? Would we be able to find our way back in a whiteout, or if snow covered our tracks? Should we be marking the route right now? Ask the questions as you go, and act on your answers. It may be a matter of think now or pay later.

Mark the Route If Necessary

There are times when it may be best to mark the route going in so you can find it again on the way out. This situation can come up when the route is over snowfields or glaciers during changeable weather, in heavy forest, or when fog or nightfall threatens to hide landmarks. On snow, climbers use thin bamboo wands with little flags to mark the path. (Chapter 8, Wilderness Routefinding, explains the construction and use of wands.) In the forest, plastic surveyor's tape is sometimes tied to branches to show the route, but we discourage its use due to its permanence, since we always endeavor to leave no trace of our passing. From an ecological standpoint, toilet paper is the best marker, because it will disintegrate during the next rainfall. Use toilet paper only if you are assured of good weather. If not, use brightly colored crepe paper in thin rolls. It will survive the next storm, but will most likely disintegrate over the winter.

One strong admonition here: *remove your markers.* Markers are litter, and good wilderness travelers never, ever litter. If there is any chance that you will not come back the same way and will not be able to remove the markers, be especially sure to use biodegradable markers.

Rock cairns appear here and there as markers, sometimes dotting an entire route and at other times signaling the point where

a route changes direction. These heaps of rock are another impo-
sition on the landscape, and they can create confusion for any
traveler but the one who put them together—so do not build them.
If there ever comes a time you decide you must, then do so, but tear
them down on the way out. The rule is different for existing cairns.
Let them be, on the assumption that someone may be depending
on them.

Keep Track

As the trip goes on, it may be helpful to mark your progress on
the map. Keep yourself oriented so that at any time you can point
out your actual position to within half a mile on the map.

Part of keeping track is having a sense of your speed. Given all
the variables, will it take your party 1 hour to travel 2 miles, or will
it take 2 hours to travel 1 mile? The answer is important if it is 3:00
P.M. and base camp is still 5 miles away. After enough trips into the
wilds, you will be good at estimating travel speeds. Here are some
typical speeds for an average party, though there will be much
variation:

- On a gentle trail, with a day pack: 2 to 3 miles per hour, or 3 to 5
  kilometers per hour
- Up a steep trail, with a full overnight pack: 1 to 2 miles per hour
- Traveling cross-country up a moderate slope, with a day pack:
  1000 feet of elevation gain per hour
- Traveling cross-country up a moderate slope, with a full
  overnight pack: 500 feet of elevation gain per hour

In heavy brush, your rate of travel can drop to a third or even a
quarter of what it would be on a good trail. Above 12,000 feet, your
rate of travel will also greatly decrease, perhaps to as little as a
hundred feet of elevation gain per hour, depending on your
condition and your state of acclimatization.

On the descent, your rate of progress can be as much as twice
as fast as on the ascent, if the terrain is easy, such as on a good trail
or a snowfield.

With a watch and a notebook (or a really good memory), you
can monitor your rate of progress on any outing. Always make sure
to note your time of starting the trip, and note the times you reach
important streams, ridges, trail junctions, and other points along
the route.

Experienced wilderness travelers regularly assess their party's
progress and compare it with the route plan. Make estimates and

re-estimates of the time when you will reach your destination, and of the time you will get back to your base camp or starting point. If it begins to look as though your party could become trapped in tricky terrain during darkness, you may decide to change your plans and bivouac in a safe place, or to call it a day and return home.

AT YOUR DESTINATION

Here is your golden opportunity to rest, relax, and enjoy—and to learn more about the area and about map reading, by comparing the actual view with the way it looks on the map. Your destination is also the place to lay final plans for the return, a journey often responsible for many more routefinding problems than the way in. Repeat the trailhead get-together by discussing the route plan and emergency strategies with everyone. Stress the importance of keeping the party together on the return. Invariably, some will want to race ahead while others lag behind.

DURING THE RETURN TRIP

The return is a time for extra caution as you fight fatigue and inattention. As on the trip in, everyone needs to maintain a good sense of the route and how it relates to the map. Stay together, do not rush, and be even more careful if you are taking a different return route.

AFTER THE TRIP

Back home, write a detailed description of the route and any problems, mistakes, or unusual features, and do it while the details are fresh in your mind. Imagine what you would like to know if you were about to do the trip for the first time, so you will be ready with the right answers when another person asks about it. If a guidebook was confusing or wrong, take the time to write to the publisher.

WHAT IF YOU *DO* GET LOST?

Why do people get lost? For a lot of reasons. Some travel without a map because the route seems obvious. Others fail to check on recent changes in roads and trails. Some folks trust their own instincts over the compass. Others do not bother with the map homework that can start them off with a good mental picture of the area. Some do not pay enough attention to the route on the way in to be able to find it on the way out. Some rely on the skill of their partner, who is just then in the process of getting them lost. Some do not think about where they are going, because they are in a hurry. Some miss junctions or wander off on game trails. Others charge mindlessly ahead despite deteriorating weather and visibility, fatigue, or flagging spirits.

Good wilderness travelers are never truly lost—but having learned humility through years of experience, they always carry enough food, clothing, and bivouac gear to get them through hours or even days of temporary confusion.

WHAT IF YOUR PARTY IS LOST?

The first rule is to *stop*. In fact, even if you *think* you might not be where you should be, *stop!* Resist the temptation to press onward. The moment you are ever unsure of your position, you should stop. Try to determine where you are. Keep your wits about you and do not forget what you have learned about map reading and using the compass. Study the shape of the terrain and try to associate it with the landscape in front of you to find out where you are. Remember the technique of the *bearing of the slope*. Take a bearing on the fall line and try to associate it with your position by studying the map. If none of these suggestions work, then try to figure out the last time the group *did* know its exact location. If that spot is fairly close, within an hour or so, retrace your steps and get back on route. But if that spot is hours back, you might instead decide to head toward the base line. If it begins to look as though darkness will fall before you can get back, you might have to bivouac for the night. If so, start looking for an adequate place, with water and firewood, well before dark.

Being lost in a party is bad enough, but it is even worse when an individual is alone and separated from the rest of the party. For this reason, always try to keep everyone together, and assign a rear guard to keep track of any stragglers. If you ever notice that a person is missing, the entire party should stop, stay together, shout, and listen for answering shouts.

WHAT IF YOU ARE LOST ALONE?

Again, the first rule is to *stop*. Look around for other members of the party, shout, and listen for answering shouts. Sound your whistle if you have one. If the only answer is silence, sit down, calm down, and combat terror with reason.

Once you have calmed down, start doing the right things. Look at your map in an attempt to determine your location, and plan a route home in case you do not connect with the rest of the party.

Mark your location with a cairn or other objects, and then scout in all directions, each time returning to your marked position. Well before dark, prepare for the night by finding water, firewood, and shelter. Staying busy will raise your spirits. Keep a fire going to give searchers something to see, and try singing (no matter how bad a singer you are) so you will have something to do and they will have something to hear.

The odds are that you will be reunited with your group by morning. If not, fight panic. After a night alone, you may decide to hike out to a base line feature you picked out before the trip—a ridge or stream or highway. If the terrain is too difficult to travel alone, it might be better to concentrate on letting yourself be found. It is far easier for rescuers to find a lost person who stays in one place in the open, builds a fire, and shouts periodically, than one who thrashes on in hysterical hope, one step ahead of the rescue party.

The decision as to whether to forge ahead or to stay put and let yourself be found is strongly influenced by whether or not anyone knows you are missing and where to look for you. If you are traveling alone, or if your entire party is lost, and no one knows you are missing or where you had planned to go, you have no choice but to try to get back yourself, even if this involves difficult travel. If, on the other hand, someone responsible expects you back at a certain time and knows where you were planning to go and what route you planned to take, then you have the option of concentrating on survival while waiting for a search party to find you.

SURVIVAL

Your chances for survival depend on how well equipped you are. Numerous stories of survival and tragedy start with statements such as, "I was sure glad I had my _____ ," or "too bad he did not bring a _____ ." Over the years these items of gear have developed into a codified list known as "The Ten Essentials." They are the following:

1. Topographic map of the area
2. Compass
3. Sunglasses and sunscreen—essential for travel on snow, to prevent snowblindness and sunburn
4. Extra food—more than you expect to eat on your trip; preferably enough to last several days
5. Extra clothing—enough to survive the coldest, wettest night you expect to encounter in the area where you will be traveling

6. Flashlight (or a headlamp, which is even better)—with extra batteries and an extra bulb
7. First-aid supplies (in case someone gets injured)—including any prescription medications that you take on a daily basis, in case you do not make it back home in time for the next dose
8. Matches (preferably waterproof, or in a waterproof container)
9. Fire-starter (for lighting wet branches)
10. Knife—preferably multipurpose, multibladed

Always consider the possibility that one member of your party might get separated from the rest of the group and will depend totally on his or her own equipment and skill for survival. This is why it is essential for each person to carry adequate food and equipment. It is equally important that each person in the party have the knowledge and skill to use all the necessary equipment (including the map and the compass), rather than always relying on the skills of another person. If someone gets lost, having the proper equipment and skills may make the difference between tragedy and a graceful recovery from the experience.

Once you have enough confidence in your abilities that you are not worried about getting lost, you are ready for off-trail navigation.

OFF-TRAIL NAVIGATION WITH MAP AND COMPASS

Getting from here to there is usually just a matter of keeping an eye on the landscape and watching where you are going, helped by an occasional glance at the map. However, if you cannot see your objective in the field, you can measure the bearing on the map, then take compass in hand and follow the direction of travel line as it guides you to the goal. This is navigation by instrument. It is a technique that will work if you are able to follow a straight-line route, something often impossible in wilderness terrain. For this reason, it is best to first try to follow topographic features in off-trail wilderness navigation, and to reserve navigation by instrument for situations where the topography lacks sufficient features to be of any help to you.

Navigation by instrument is sometimes the only practical method for finding a crucial pass, base camp, or other goal. It also serves as a supplement to other methods, such as following topographic features, and it can help to verify that you are on the right track. Again, use common sense and challenge a compass reading that defies reason. (Is your declination arrow or direction of travel line pointing the wrong way, sending you 180 degrees off course?)

MAP AND COMPASS

The most common situation requiring instrument navigation comes when the route is unclear because the topography is featureless or because landmarks are obscured by forest or fog. You do know exactly where you are and exactly where you want to go and can identify both your present position and your destination on the map. In this case, simply measure the bearing from your present position to your objective on the map, then follow that bearing to your objective. Suppose you measure a bearing of 285 degrees on the map (fig. 18a). Read this bearing at the index line and leave it set there (fig. 18b). Then hold your compass out in front of you as you rotate your body until you have "boxed" the needle. The direction of travel line now points to your objective (fig. 18c). Start walking.

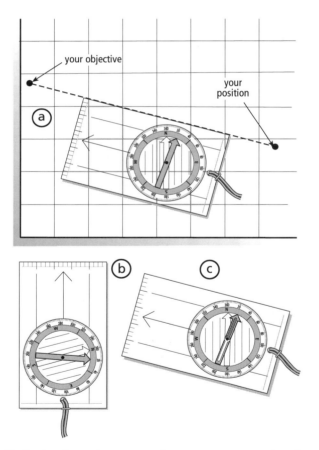

Figure 18. Navigation using map and compass: a. measuring the bearing on the map; b. bearing at index line; c. following the bearing ("box" the needle). Magnetic needle not shown in a and b.

COMPASS ALONE

Navigators of air and ocean often travel by instrument alone; so can you. For example, suppose you are scrambling toward a pass and clouds begin to obscure your view of it. Just take a quick compass bearing on the pass before it disappears from view. Then follow that bearing, compass in hand if you wish. You do not even have to note the numerical bearing; just "box" the needle and keep it boxed as you proceed to your objective. Likewise, if you are heading into a valley where fog or forest will hide your goal, take a bearing on the goal before you drop into the valley, and then follow that bearing after you lose sight of the objective (fig. 19). This method becomes more reliable if several people travel together, checking each other's work by taking occasional back bearings on each other.

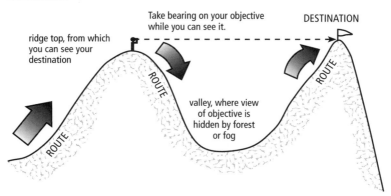

Figure 19. Following a compass bearing when the view of the objective will be obscured by forest or fog

USING INTERMEDIATE OBJECTIVES

A handy technique is available for those frustrating times when you try to travel exactly along a compass bearing but keep getting diverted by obstructions such as cliffs, dense brush, or crevasses. Try the technique of *intermediate objectives*. If in a forest, sight past the obstruction to a tree or rock or other object that is exactly on the bearing line to the principal objective (fig. 20a). Then you are free to travel over to the tree or rock by whatever route is easiest. When you get to the intermediate objective, you can be confident that you are still on the correct route. This technique is useful even when there is no obstruction. Moving from one intermediate objective to another means you can put the compass away for those stretches,

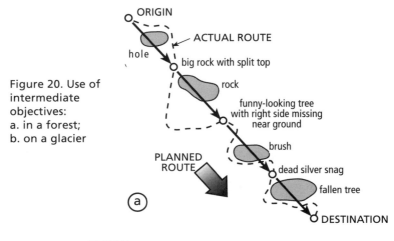

Figure 20. Use of
intermediate
objectives:
a. in a forest;
b. on a glacier

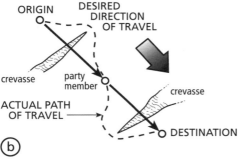

rather than having to hold it continually in your hand and check it
every few steps.

Sometimes on snow or glaciers, in fog, or in a forest where all
the trees look the same, there are no natural intermediate objectives.
In this case, another member of the party can serve as the target
(fig. 20b). Send that person out to near the limit of visibility or past
the obstruction. Wave this person left or right until he or she is
directly on the bearing line. That person can improve the accuracy
of the route by taking a back bearing on you.

THE INTENTIONAL OFFSET ("AIMING OFF")

Now imagine that your party is almost back to the car after a
scramble. You follow a compass bearing to the logging road, but
you cannot see the car because you are off route by a few degrees.
You have to guess which way to go. It is a bad ending to the trip if
the car is to the right and you go left. It will be even worse if the car

is parked at the *end* of the road, and a routefinding error takes the party beyond that point and on and on through the woods (fig. 21a). The *intentional offset* (also called "aiming off") was invented for this situation (fig. 21b). Just travel in a direction that is intentionally offset by 20 to 30 degrees to the right or the left of wherever you want to be. When you hit the road, there will be no doubt about which way to turn.

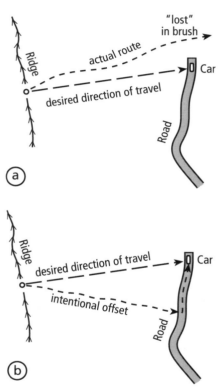

Figure 21. Navigating to a specific point on a line: a. inevitable minor errors can sometimes have disastrous consequences; b. to avoid such problems, follow a course with an intentional offset.

NAVIGATING AROUND AN OBSTRUCTION

Sometimes you try to follow a constant bearing to get to your objective, but find that the route is blocked by an obstruction such as a lake or a cliff. There may be an easy way to get around the obstruction, but doing so forces you off your intended bearing. What do you do?

If the obstruction is a lake or swamp, you may be able to see across it back to your starting point after you have traveled past it

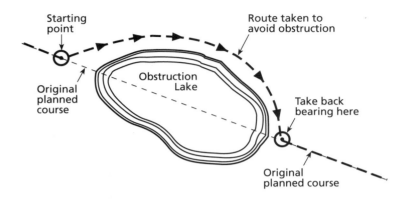

Figure 22. Navigating around an obstruction when you can see across the obstruction once you are past it *(Illustration by J. Shontz)*

(fig. 22). In this case, try to find some large, easily visible object on your bearing line before you start traveling past the obstruction. If that point is a nondescript location with no identifiable landmark, you can mark this spot with a streamer of toilet paper or other material which will rapidly deteriorate in the next storm. Once you know that you have an identifiable object or marker along your bearing line, you can walk around the obstruction using whatever route is easiest. Once past the obstruction, take a back bearing on your starting point. If this does not match the bearing of your intended direction of travel, then continue around the obstruction until your back bearing on the starting point matches your intended direction of travel.

If the obstruction is a cliff, mountain, or other feature which prevents you from seeing your starting point once you have passed the obstruction, then you may have to use a different technique, as shown in figure 23. In this case, you can travel a paced distance at 90 degrees to the original course, then go past the blockage on a bearing parallel to the original course, and finally return to the original course by another 90-degree course change paced the same distance as the earlier one, but in the opposite direction.

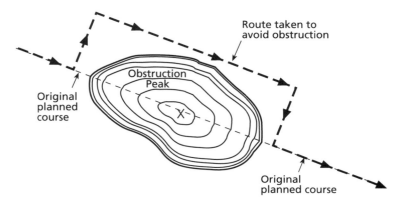

Figure 23. Navigating around an obstruction when the view across the obstruction is blocked *(Illustration by J. Shontz)*

A REMINDER

At the start of this chapter we recommended using topographic features whenever possible in off-trail navigation and using navigation by instrument only for those situations in which the topography lacks sufficient features to help you. Now, after describing six different techniques used in off-trail navigation, we are concerned that you might have forgotten the original point, so we will repeat it: wherever possible, navigate by using natural topographic features. Reserve the use of navigation by instrument for those situations where there is no alternative. This applies not only to the compass but also to other instruments such as the altimeter.

THE ALTIMETER

The altimeter, like a compass, provides one simple piece of information that forms the basis for a tremendous amount of vital detail: it gives the elevation. By monitoring the elevation and checking it against the topographic map, wilderness travelers can keep track of their progress, pinpoint their location, and find their way to critical junctions on the route. The altimeter is little help in the plains, where there is little or no change in elevation. But in mountainous terrain, it can be a great help in orientation, navigation, and routefinding.

WHAT THE ALTIMETER IS AND HOW IT WORKS

An altimeter is basically a modified barometer. Both instruments measure air pressure (the weight of air). A barometer indicates air pressure on a scale calibrated in inches or millimeters of mercury, or in millibars. An altimeter is scaled to read out in feet or meters above or below sea level—which is possible because air pressure decreases at a predictable rate with increasing altitude.

TYPES OF ALTIMETERS

The most popular wilderness altimeter is the digital type, combined with a watch and worn on the wrist (fig. 24a). The digital wristwatch altimeter has several advantages over the analog type (fig. 24b). Some digital altimeters display additional information, such as the temperature and the rate of altitude gain or loss. Since most people wear a watch anyway, this type of altimeter is helpful because it combines multiple functions into one piece of equipment. The altimeter worn on the wrist is more convenient to use than one

Figure 24. Typical altimeters: a. digital wristwatch type; b. analog type

kept in a pocket or pack and therefore will be consulted more frequently.

A disadvantage of the digital type is that it requires a battery—which can die out or become temporarily disconnected due to mechanical shock, causing all its data to be lost. It can also fail if water gets into the mechanism. The liquid-crystal display (LCD) usually goes blank at temperatures below about 0° F (-18° C), making it essential to keep the instrument relatively warm. (This is usually not a problem as long as you keep the altimeter on your wrist. If it gets cold enough for the LCD to go blank, the altimeter still retains all its data and will display the data properly once it gets warm enough for the display to work.) But when starting a technical rock-climbing pitch, it is a good idea to remove the altimeter from your wrist and attach it to your pack strap or put in into your pack to keep it from getting banged up on the rock or stuck in a crack.

The analog altimeter has the advantages of being a simpler instrument than a digital one, requiring no battery, and working at temperatures well below zero. To read an analog altimeter, begin by holding it level in the palm of one hand. Look directly down on the needle, your eyes at least a foot above it, to reduce errors due to viewing angle. Tap it lightly several times to overcome any slight friction in the mechanism.

EFFECTS OF WEATHER ON ALTIMETERS

The accuracy of an altimeter depends on the weather, because a change in the weather is usually accompanied by a change in air pressure, which can cause an error in the altimeter reading. A change in barometric pressure of 1 inch of mercury corresponds to a change in altitude of roughly 1000 feet. If you are in camp during a day in which the air pressure increases by two-tenths of an inch (for example, from 30.00 to 30.20 inches), your altimeter will show a reading about 200 feet less than it was at the beginning of the day, even though you have remained in the same place. If you had gone out on a hike during that same day, your elevation readings by the end of the day would likewise have been about 200 feet low. During periods of unstable weather, your indicated elevation may change by as much as 500 feet in one day although your actual elevation has remained the same. Even during apparently stable conditions, an erroneous indicated change in elevation of 100 feet per day is not uncommon.

EFFECTS OF TEMPERATURE ON ALTIMETERS

The altimeter sensor expands and contracts due to variations in temperature, causing changes in the indicated elevation. A bimetallic element in *temperature-compensated* altimeters adjusts for this effect *when there is no actual change in elevation*. When you are gaining or losing elevation, however, this compensation is sometimes not enough, resulting in errors even in altimeters that are temperature-compensated. To minimize the effects of temperature changes, try to keep the altimeter's temperature as constant as possible. Body heat will usually accomplish this with a wristwatch altimeter, particularly if it is worn under a parka when the outside temperature is low. With an analog altimeter, you can keep its temperature relatively constant by carrying it in your pocket rather than in your pack.

PRECISION AND ACCURACY

Because even the most precise and costly altimeters are strongly influenced by the weather, do not be misled into trusting them to a degree of accuracy that is greater than possible. A typical high-quality altimeter may have a precision (smallest marked division of an analog instrument, or smallest indicated change of a digital one) of 10 or 20 feet. This does not mean the altimeter will always be that accurate. Changes in weather could easily throw the reading off by hundreds of feet. Get to know your altimeter, use it often, check it at every opportunity, and note differences of opinion between it and the map. You will soon learn just what level of accuracy to expect, and your altimeter will then be a dependable aid to roving the wilds.

USING THE ALTIMETER IN WILDERNESS TRAVEL

Because of the strong influence of weather on an altimeter's accuracy, you cannot trust the instrument until you first set it at a known elevation. Then it is important when you are traveling to check the reading whenever you reach another point of known elevation so you can reset it if necessary.

ORIENTATION

An altimeter can be a big help in determining exactly where you are. If you are climbing a ridge or hiking up a trail shown on the map, but you do not know exactly where you are along the ridge or trail, check the altimeter for the elevation. Where the ridge or trail reaches that contour line on the map is your likely location.

Another way to get the altimeter to tell you where you are is to start with a compass bearing to a summit or some other known feature. Find that peak on the map and plot the bearing line from the mountain back toward your approximate location. This gives you line position; you know you must be somewhere along this line. But where? Take an altimeter reading and find out the elevation. Where the compass bearing line crosses a contour line at this elevation is your likely location. This could lead to an ambiguous answer, of course, because the bearing line might cross that contour line at several points. Then you turn to further observations (such as slope direction, topography, and vegetation), common sense, and intuition.

NAVIGATION

Navigation gets easier with an altimeter. If you top a convenient couloir at 9400 feet and gain the ridge you want to ascend, make a note of that elevation in a notebook or on the map. On the way back, descend the ridge to that elevation and you should easily find the couloir again.

Guidebook descriptions sometimes specify a change of direction at a particular elevation. If you are on an open snowfield or a forested hillside, good luck in making the turn at the right place without an altimeter. The route you have worked out on a topographic map also may depend on course changes at certain elevations, and again the altimeter will keep your party on target.

DECISION MAKING

The altimeter helps in deciding whether to continue a trip or to turn back, by letting you calculate your rate of ascent. Suppose you have been keeping an hourly check on time and elevation during a hike. It has taken the party four hours to ascend 3000 feet, an average of 750 feet per hour. But you know that the actual rate of ascent has been declining with each hour. In fact, the party gained only 500 feet in the past hour, compared with 1000 feet in the first hour. You know that the destination is at an elevation of 8400 feet, and an altimeter reading shows you are now at 6400. So you can predict that it will take roughly four more hours to reach your destination. Take that information, courtesy of the altimeter, combine it with a look at the weather, the time of the day, and the condition of party members, and you have the data on which to base a sound decision as to whether to proceed with the trip or turn back.

PREDICTING THE WEATHER

The altimeter can help in predicting the weather. The readings on an altimeter and on a barometer operate in opposition to one another. When one goes up, the other goes down. An altimeter reading showing an increase in elevation when no actual elevation change has taken place (such as at camp overnight) means a falling barometer, which often predicts deteriorating weather. A decreasing altimeter reading, on the other hand, means increasing barometric pressure and possibly improving weather. This is an oversimplification, of course; weather forecasting is complicated by the wind, local weather peculiarities, and the rate of barometric pressure change. Make frequent observations of altimeter readings and weather patterns on your trips—and even while at home—if you want to figure out the relationship between weather and altimeter readings in your particular geographic area.

Some digital wristwatch altimeters can be adjusted to read barometric pressure instead of altitude. But keep in mind that changes in barometric pressure are useful in assessing the weather only when the readings are taken at a constant elevation (such as in camp). Using the altimeter as a barometer while you are ascending or descending will give readings that are influenced not only by changes in barometric pressure but also by changes in your elevation as you travel. Your conclusions about barometric pressure trends may be erroneous under such circumstances.

On extended trips, it is often a good idea to keep track of barometric pressure trends at camps. Be sure to reset the altimeter at known elevations, then record pressure or altitude readings in your notebook or journal, along with notes about weather conditions, such as whether it is raining, snowing, windy, sunny, etc. By documenting pressure trends and weather patterns you will learn how to predict future weather based on past observations. This works best at fixed camps at known elevations.

USE OF BEARING OF THE SLOPE WITH THE ALTIMETER

The *bearing of the slope* becomes a very powerful tool when combined with altimeter use. Sometimes, when on a featureless snow slope, in a dense forest, or in foggy conditions, it is impossible to take bearings on visible landmarks and there are no identifiable topographic features for you to compare with the map. Under these and similar conditions, knowing your altitude plus the bearing of the slope can often provide you with enough information to enable you to determine your position with a high degree of certainty. In fact, in the absence of definite topographic features or visible landmarks, the use of the altimeter plus the bearing of the slope might well be the *only* way to determine your position, unless you have a GPS receiver.

THE GLOBAL POSITIONING SYSTEM (GPS)

Global positioning system (GPS) receivers (fig. 25) have gained wide acceptance among sailors, arctic explorers, surveyors, and others for many years. They have recently become small and affordable enough to use in wilderness navigation. Most weigh less than a pound and can fit in a jacket pocket. GPS receivers range in cost from about $100 to $1000, depending on features.

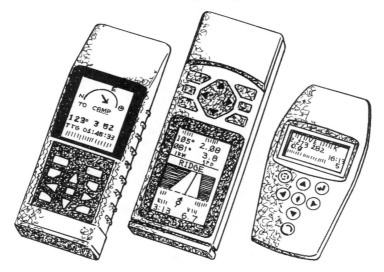

Figure 25. Different types of GPS receivers

HOW THE GPS WORKS

The U.S. Department of Defense has placed twenty-four GPS satellites into orbit. These satellites continuously broadcast position and timing information to every point on the earth. A small, hand-held, portable GPS receiver can acquire signals from these satellites to provide position and altitude.

GPS receivers have a basic accuracy of about 50 feet (15 meters). However, the Department of Defense can (and often does) degrade this accuracy to prevent its use by perceived enemies. This degradation is called *selective availability* (SA). When SA is in effect, GPS point position accuracy is degraded by approximately 300 feet (or approximately 100 meters). This degree of accuracy is often sufficient to find your way back to a large trailhead parking lot. However, it is not adequate for use in detailed routefinding where route changes may involve finding features only a few yards in size.

USING GPS IN WILDERNESS TRAVEL

The most useful function of the GPS is to tell you your position (i.e., orientation). The GPS receiver is turned on, and within a few minutes the signals are acquired (if you have an adequate view of the sky). The receiver then displays your location in latitude and longitude, or in UTM coordinates, and you can find this position on your map.

The GPS receiver can also tell you the direction and distance to your objective (i.e., navigation). If your destination is shown on the map but you cannot see it in the field, you can enter the map coordinates of your objective into the GPS receiver. The receiver can then tell you the distance and compass bearing to that objective. Once you are walking, the receiver can tell you the actual bearing you are following, your speed, and other navigational information. If you are not heading directly toward your objective, the receiver can tell you which way to turn until you are again on the desired route.

Most GPS receivers have a *waypoint* (sometimes called *land-mark*) feature as an aid in navigation. Waypoints, or landmarks, are positions along the route that can be entered into the receiver's memory. You can either store your present position, as determined by the GPS receiver, or the position of a feature on your map, as read off the map in latitude and longitude or UTM coordinates. Imagine leaving camp in good weather but reaching your desti-nation just as thick clouds roll in. Luckily, you have been setting waypoints all morning at crucial route junctures. With a few deliberate keystrokes from you, the GPS receiver leads you back to camp, waypoint by waypoint.

GPS receivers have some obvious advantages over magnetic compasses. A compass can tell you your position only if you can see landmarks and can take bearings on them. The GPS receiver, on the other hand, can tell your position (usually to within a sphere of uncertainty roughly the size of a football field) *without any visible landmarks*. This can be particularly helpful in fog or a whiteout, or in featureless terrain.

In chapter 5 we described various strategies to use to follow a compass bearing toward your objective, such as the use of intermediate objectives and detouring a paced distance around an obstruction. When using a compass, such techniques are essential if you wish to stay on your correct course. With a GPS receiver, however, navigation becomes easier. If you are trying to follow a given bearing to your destination and the route is blocked, you can simply travel around the blockage by the easiest route, not worrying about how far off route you get, or in what direction. Once past the obstruction, you can again turn on your GPS receiver, obtain a new position, and get the receiver to tell you the *new* bearing to your objective. Then you can set that new bearing on your compass and follow it.

When planning a wilderness trip, you should find the coordinates of critical sites (e.g., the starting point, the destination, and other crucial points) on the map and enter them into the GPS receiver as waypoints. This can easily be done at home before the trip.

One of the most useful ways of using a GPS receiver is *in addition to* (rather than *instead of*) using your compass. For example, you can establish your position and your destination as waypoints and get the GPS receiver to tell you the distance and compass bearing to your destination. Then you can set this bearing on your magnetic compass and use your compass to travel at the correct bearing, with the GPS receiver turned off to save battery power. During these times you can also place the GPS receiver safely in your pack, protecting it from harm as you travel with your compass as a guide. This technique has been used, for example, by parties crossing the featureless inland ice of Greenland. The GPS receiver is turned on several times a day, to establish position and to determine the bearing to the objective. The rest of the time it is turned off and put away. This practice saves considerable battery power when compared to traveling with the GPS receiver turned on all of the time. It is also more convenient to travel without having to hold the GPS receiver in your hand all the time. You may want to use that hand for holding an ice ax or a ski pole, or for climbing over trees or rocks.

USE OF GPS WITH UTM COORDINATE SYSTEM

Using the GPS is easiest if the map is overlaid with a grid of UTM coordinates, as described in chapter 1. UTM is a grid of 1-kilometer squares. The distance between UTM coordinate lines is 1000 meters (or 3281 feet, or 1094 yards, or 0.6214 miles). It is fairly easy to "eyeball" the position of any point on the map to one-tenth of the UTM grid coordinates, even without a ruler. This will get you to within about 100 meters of the correct position. With the Defense Department's "selective availability" in effect, 100 meters is about as close to the correct position as the GPS receiver will get you anyway. If your map does not have UTM coordinate lines, it should at least have tick marks on the map's borders that indicate the locations of the UTM 1000-meter coordinate lines. You can then draw in the UTM lines at home before your trip, using a pencil and a yardstick (as described in chapter 1). This greatly simplifies GPS navigation.

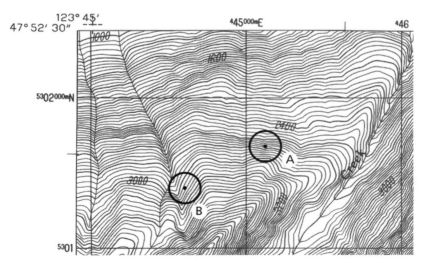

Figure 26. Use of the UTM coordinate system with GPS receivers
(Illustration by J. Shontz)

Figure 26 shows a portion of a 7.5-minute topographic map with UTM lines. UTM coordinates are defined in terms of *eastings* and *northings*: the distances, in meters, east and north of a reference point for one of sixty *zones* around the earth. The zone number is given in the lower left corner of the topographic map. For example, the map used in figure 26 says "GRID: 1000-METER UNIVERSAL TRANSVERSE MERCATOR. . . . ZONE 10" in its lower left corner.

At the top of the map is the number 4 45 000mE. This is called the *full easting* (except for zone) and shows that this line is 445,000 meters east of the reference line for Zone 10. To its right is the number 4 46. This is a *partial easting*, with the "000" meters not included. This line is 446,000 meters east of the Zone 10 reference line.

Suppose we want to read the coordinates of point *A* off the map, so that we can enter this spot into the GPS receiver as a waypoint. Point *A* is about 1/10 of the way between the eastings of 4 45 000 and 4 46 000. Its easting is therefore 10 4 45 100E. (The "10" in front of the easting indicates the *zone*.)

Along the left edge of the map, you can see the *full northing* of 53 02 000mN. This line is 5,302,000 meters north of the equator. One kilometer below this line is another line identified as "53 01." This is a *partial northing*, with the "000" meters not included.

In the north-south direction, point *A* is about 7/10 of the way between the northings of 53 01 000 and 53 02 000, so the northing of point *A* is 53 01 700N. You could therefore enter the following UTM coordinates into your GPS receiver as a waypoint for point *A*:

10 4 45 100E
53 01 700N

You should be able to see that point B is about 6/10 of the way between the eastings of 4 44 000 and 4 45 000, so the easting of this point is estimated to be 10 4 44 600E (again, the "10" is for the zone). The northing of point B is about 4/10 of the way between 53 01 000 and 53 02 000, so its northing can be estimated to be 53 01 400N.

If you were to go to the point indicated by point B and let your GPS receiver acquire a position, it would read about:

10 4 44 600E
53 01 400N

Note: We have drawn the circles at points A and B to have a radius of 100 meters, so that the borders of the circles are 100 meters from the coordinates given. This corresponds to the 100-meter accuracy of the GPS receiver under most conditions when SA is in effect. This shows how close you can expect your indicated GPS position to be (the "sphere of uncertainty").

If you have difficulty "eyeballing" distances between UTM coordinate lines, there are several types of rulers and other measuring devices that you can use instead. You can purchase small plastic scales to read UTM coordinates on 1:24,000-scale (7.5-minute) maps, but this means carrying one more piece of special equipment. Some compasses are equipped with special scales to locate your position on 1:24,000 maps; some of these have "GPS" in their model numbers. Some other compasses have "roamer" (sometimes spelled "romer") scales for use with either 1:24,000 or 1:25,000 scale maps. USGS 7.5-minute maps have a scale of 1:24,000, so that is the scale you should use. However, if your compass has a roamer scale for use with 1:25,000 maps, that is close enough to 1:24,000 that you can use it anyway, with only minimal error.

DATUMS, ZONES, AND BANDS

The *map datum* is a reference that is usually found in the lower left corner of the topographic map. Several different ones are in use: WGS (World Geodetic System) 84, NAD (North American Datum) 1927, NAD 1983, and others. Before using your GPS receiver, you should find this datum on your map, then go to the GPS receiver's setup screen and set the datum to agree with your map. Using the wrong datum will give you positions which are consistently wrong by the same distance.

The UTM *zone* can usually be found on maps that include UTM lines or grid ticks. There are sixty UTM zones around the world, each six degrees wide. Zone 1 is for the area from 180° W to 174° W, and its zone meridian (centerline) is 177° W. Zone 2 is to the east of zone 1: from 174° W to 168° W, with a zone meridian of 171° W. From this you should be able to figure out the zone of any longitude on the earth if you have to. The centerline of each zone is numbered 5 00 000mE.

Some GPS receivers use a "latitude band" with UTM to indicate position relative to the equator. This system divides the earth into eight-degree-wide latitude bands from 80° S latitude to 84° N latitude (the northernmost band being a bit wider than the others). The bands are lettered from south to north, according to the following table:

Latitude Bands and Latitude Ranges

Lat. Band	Lat. Range	Lat. Band	Lat. Range
C	72–80 South	N	0–8 North
D	64–72 South	P	8–16 North
E	56–64 South	Q	16–24 North
F	48–56 South	R	24–32 North
G	40–48 South	S	32–40 North
H	32–40 South	T	40–48 North
J	24–32 South	U	48–56 North
K	16–24 South	V	56–64 North
L	8–16 South	W	64–72 North
M	0–8 South	X	72–84 North

If the latitude band is used, the letter for that band is placed immediately after the zone number. Some GPS receivers require using such a latitude band. Others merely ask you to tell it which hemisphere you are in, north or south. Due to distortion of the UTM grid lines near the poles, UTM is not defined north of 84° N or south of 80° S latitude. The area covered by UTM includes most of the world except Antarctica and arctic regions north of Alaska's north coast. In those areas, UTM cannot be used, but you can use latitude and longitude or the Universal Polar Stereographic (UPS) grid instead.

CAUTIONS ABOUT THE USE OF GPS RECEIVERS

As marvelous as they are, GPS receivers have a few drawbacks. One major problem is that GPS receivers may not be able to pick up adequate satellite signals while under heavy forest cover, in deep canyons or gullies, or on a steep hillside. In this case, you must either move to an open area or use conventional map and compass techniques. Inexpensive two-channel receivers are the most subject to this problem. The more expensive eight-channel and twelve-channel receivers perform much better under these circumstances.

Another problem with GPS receivers is that they occasionally indicate the wrong position. Selective availability, as explained above, is one reason for this sort of error. A small proportion (less than 5%) of the time, the receiver's indicated position may be more than 100 meters away from the actual position. (We refer to such points as "outliers.") In addition, some conditions of low signal strength or poor geometric quality of the signals received may be to blame. This can happen in an area of heavy forest cover or in a narrow gully, or in any area in which the satellites are not in good enough positions to give you trustworthy information. Signal reflections off buildings or cliffs can also cause errors. In some cases, the receiver tells you of the problem by means of blinking readouts, audible warnings, or special "icons" or messages on the display. If any of these conditions is indicated, you should disregard the coordinates of the displayed signal, and should not save the acquired position for use in any route, nor use it in a "Go To" command. These problems are the most severe with two-channel receivers.

The conditions leading to these kinds of position errors are sometimes only temporary, often not lasting more than a minute or two. To overcome this condition, you should not merely use the first position that your receiver displays. Instead, watch the display to ensure that the displayed position is stable and not varying by more than plus or minus 100 meters. If you really need an accurate position, it is very important to watch the display for a few minutes to make sure that you are not using an outlier in your route.

If you decide to purchase a GPS receiver, we recommend that you carefully study the models available, talk to GPS users, read magazine articles, and do other research to decide which model is best for you. We recommend a good eight- or twelve-channel unit rather than one of the cheapest two-channel receivers. Do not be misled by advertising or catalog data such as "tracks twelve channels," since two-channel receivers do this, but not simultaneously. (Two-channel receivers can track twelve satellites, but only by time-sharing between them. While switching from one to another, a momentary loss of a signal from one satellite, such as from heavy foliage, can cause such a receiver to completely lose its position fix.) Look for a receiver whose specifications state that there are eight or twelve *parallel* channels. Another useful feature is automatic averaging, in which successive position fixes are averaged until you save your position. Using such a feature and waiting for several minutes can overcome the effects of SA and out-liers to a great extent, since occasional outliers and normal position errors will be averaged, providing a more accurate position.

A refinement of the GPS called *differential* GPS (DGPS) can provide much more accurate position information, but DGPS usage is more complex, more expensive, and heavier, because it requires a unit called a "differential beacon receiver" in addition to a "differential ready" receiver. For most wilderness navigation purposes, DGPS is not necessary, since knowing your position to within 100 meters is usually adequate.

Some magazine articles and advertising have suggested that GPS receivers will make magnetic compasses obsolete. This probably will not happen, however, for a long time, since the two instruments do not have the same function. GPS receivers provide *position* information, while compasses provide *direction*. Some of the higher-priced GPS receivers contain built-in compasses, but most do not. Even when carrying a receiver with a built-in compass, however, you should always also carry a magnetic compass, in case of a malfunction of the GPS receiver, and for measuring and plotting bearings on a map.

A GPS receiver is no substitute for a good altimeter, because the GPS altitude information is nowhere near as accurate as that provided by the altimeter. In addition, an altimeter can provide barometric pressure information, which is not available from a GPS receiver.

This chapter is intended only as a *supplement* to the information given in your GPS receiver's instruction manual. If you get a GPS receiver, it is essential that you read the instruction manual carefully to learn every aspect of the receiver's operation, and that you practice using it to master its operation *before* you depend on it in the wilderness. Go to a place whose coordinates can be found on a map and compare the GPS receiver readout to the coordinates you read on the map. Then watch the display for up to half an hour to observe the stability and repeatability of the readout and to see outliers if they occur. Try your receiver in various conditions of heavy forest cover, in gullies and canyons, and along steep hillsides. Again, it is best to find out how much you can trust your GPS receiver *before* relying on it in the wilderness.

We highly recommended that you never get yourself into a position of complete dependence on a GPS receiver. You should always have a reliable backup method of navigation in case the GPS receiver fails. This backup method usually consists of a map and a compass, plus the knowledge of how to use them. If you ever envision a wilderness travel situation in which you will truly be relying on GPS navigation to get you to your destination or back (e.g., when crossing Greenland), then you should plan on carrying at least *two* GPS receivers, so that you will be able to navigate even if one fails, or is damaged or lost. Furthermore, we strongly suggest that you always use the GPS receiver as a *supplement* to conventional navigation techniques, rather than as a complete replacement. For example, if you are climbing a glaciated peak with a GPS receiver, you might be tempted not to place wands, relying instead on the GPS receiver to find your way back. What would you do if a whiteout occurred and your GPS receiver failed, or its batteries went dead? And remember that you might encounter some conditions of heavy forest cover and/or topography in which even the best receiver might be unable to provide a position fix.

The GPS receiver is a delicate, complex, battery-powered electronic device that does not always prevail over the rigors of the wilderness. The lower temperature limit for GPS receivers ranges from -4° F (-20° C) to +32° F (0° C), depending on the model. If you plan on using one in extremely cold conditions, be sure to check its specifications carefully when choosing which one to buy. Also, you should carry the GPS receiver in an inside pocket or some other place where it will be kept reasonably warm.

GPS receivers can also be damaged by dropping them or stepping on them, or accidentally bumping them into hard surfaces. They are more complicated to use than magnetic compasses, and because they operate on battery power, the length of time that you can use them is limited. You should always carry a spare set of batteries for your GPS receiver.

A GPS receiver cannot replace conventional map and compass techniques. Compasses work at temperatures well below zero, require no batteries, and are so simple that there is very little that can go wrong with them. In addition, they are so lightweight and inexpensive that every party member can carry one. They are easy to operate and understand, and all function in even the thickest of forests. The map and compass remain the cornerstones of navigation and wilderness routefinding.

WILDERNESS ROUTEFINDING

Routefinding begins at home. Before heading out the door, you need to know not only the name of your wilderness destination but also a great deal about how to get there. The information is accessible to anyone who takes the trouble to seek it out, from guidebooks and maps and from people who have been there.

Prepare for each trip as if you were going to lead it, even if you are not. Each person in the group needs to know wilderness navigation and must keep track of where the party has been, where it is, and where it is going. In case of an emergency, each party member must be able to get back, alone.

Guidebooks provide critical information such as a description of the route, the estimated time necessary to complete it, elevation gain, distance, and so forth. Travelers who have previously made the trip may be able to tell you about landmarks, hazards, and routefinding hassles. Useful details are packed into maps of all sorts: Forest Service maps, road maps, aerial maps, sketch maps, and topographic maps. For a trip into an area that is particularly unfamiliar to you, more preparation is needed. This might include scouting into the area, observations from distant vantage points, or a study of aerial photographs.

If the route comes from a guidebook or from a description provided by another person, plot it out on the topographic map you will be carrying, noting trail junctions and other important points. It can help to highlight the route with a yellow felt-tip marking pen, which does not obliterate map features. Additional maps or route descriptions should be taken, along with the topo map, marked with notes on any more up-to-date information. In selecting the route, consider a host of factors, including the season, weather conditions, the abilities of party members, and the equipment available.

Before you have even shouldered your pack, you should have a mental image of the route. From experience, and from all the sources of information about the trip, you should know how to make the terrain work in your favor. A rock slide area can be a feasible route, providing that you watch for new rockfall. One problem in planning your route, however, is that a rock slide area may look the same on a map as an avalanche gully, which can be an avalanche hazard in winter and spring and choked with brush in summer and fall. If your information sources are not helpful, only a firsthand look will clear up this question.

The most straightforward return route is often the same as the route going in. To minimize the possibility of getting off track, it is usually best to return by the same route as on the way to your objective. If you plan to come back a different way, then that route also needs careful advance preparation.

You should not let outdated information ruin your trip. Check beforehand with the appropriate agencies about roads and trails, especially closures, and also about off-trail routes, regulations, permits, and camping requirements.

ON THE TRAIL

When following trails, be sure to make note of all trail junctions. Some are indistinct, unmarked, or obscure. Others, though marked with signs, are easy to miss if you are in a hurry or not paying close attention. When following a good trail through nondescript territory, it is easy to get into a form of mental autopilot, in which you just keep on walking without taking much note of features you are passing. In such conditions, it is easy to miss trail junctions and wander off onto the wrong trail. Try to avoid this by keeping alert to your surroundings and always searching for trail junctions and other noteworthy features.

Wherever possible—at clearings in the forest, trail junctions, stream crossings, passes, and other locations that you can identify on the map—you should pay attention to when you reach such places, and find them on the map. Be observant of the topography that you pass. For example, you may see a ridge or a gully coming down a mountainside, and you can glance at your map to note that you are passing such a feature. In addition to helping you to keep track of your position, this practice will eventually make you an expert map reader.

When traveling in a group, it is easy to get spread out along the trail, since it is seldom that everyone in a party will walk at the same pace. However, this occasionally leads to people getting separated from the rest of the group and sometimes getting lost. For this reason, it is critically important to stop and wait for stragglers from time to time, at all trail junctions and other places where it might be possible for someone to go astray. If you come to a place where the trail becomes indistinct or otherwise hard to follow, it is essential to stop and wait for all members of the party to catch up. At the beginning of a hike, and at various places along the way, the leader should instruct everybody to stop and wait at certain bridges, trail junctions, or other obvious places until the whole group catches up.

When the trail gets lost in snow, blowdown, or overgrown brush, there are ways to find and stay on the trail other than just following a well-beaten path. One way is to look for *blazes* on trees—slashes, usually made by an ax—normally about 6 feet or so above ground level. Another telltale sign is the *prunings* that occasionally are visible, where tree limbs have been cut during trail maintenance operations. And if neither of these helps you to stay on the trail, ask yourself, "Where would I go if I were a trail?" Trail builders usually locate trails on the easiest terrain, with a minimum of ups and downs, and with the least amount of effort. Remembering this may help you to re-locate the trail. If you do lose the trail in brush, woods, or snow, then you should immediately stop, retrace your steps, and locate the last known trail position. It is often tempting to keep pressing on, with the notion that the trail will eventually emerge. But this is rarely the case. Go back and find the trail and then start the process of finding the true route to your destination, whether back on the original trail or by some other route.

Even if the trail is muddy or full of puddles, we strongly recommend that you stay on the trail, walking right through the puddles, even if this means getting your feet wet. (The inconvenience of this practice is lessened by wearing appropriate footwear: good, solid, waterproofed boots, which will not soak through when you walk through water.) Walking off the trail to find dry spots eventually creates multiple parallel paths and causes a severe human impact on the wilderness. In addition, we recommend that you be careful not to damage trailside vegetation—for example, by taking rest stops at places with rocks or logs, or at open, bare areas for you to stop and take your pack off, rather than at places where you might damage trailside vegetation. (It may be argued that such considerations are not relevant to wilderness navigation. However, if we destroy or severely damage the wilderness by our human impact, the whole subject of wilderness navigation could someday become irrelevant.)

IN THE FOREST

The moment you step off the road or trail and enter the forest, you should remind yourself that you are leaving your handrail, and you need to look for another one. The new handrail could be a topographic feature, such as a ridge, gully, or stream. In the total absence of real, physical handrails, you can conceivably follow an invisible, abstract, handrail such as a contour line (by keeping level, neither gaining nor losing elevation) or a compass bearing. If you do this, be sure to make a note of the elevation or bearing that you are following. Never merely wander off into the woods with no clear idea of the direction in which you are headed. You will also need a new base line; this might be the road or trail that was your previous handrail.

It is best to try to follow topographic features when choosing a route in the forest. To avoid heavy brush, try to follow ridges and dense, old-growth timber, if you can find it. Gullies, watercourses, and second growth may be choked with lush, difficult vegetation. You may encounter remnants of trails from time to time. If so, take advantage of them, since doing so may save you time and energy. But keep in mind that the destination of such a trail may well be different from yours. So if the trail starts to deviate from your intended direction of travel too much, be prepared to leave it and head back to off-trail travel.

It may sound self-evident and trite, but you should always remember that if you know where you are, you are not lost. So always keep track of your position using topography, time, vegetation, elevation, and any other means at your disposal. Perhaps you headed off into the woods at a bearing of 250 degrees for an hour, till you reached an elevation of 3500 feet as indicated on your altimeter. Then you traversed level terrain at a bearing of 310 degrees in open terrain. Then you ascended a forested ridge until you reached a broad bench at 4800 feet. Be sure to consult the map at frequent intervals to find each topographic feature that you encounter. Record your route in your notebook or on your map. The route will look entirely different on your return, but with the aid of your map, compass, notebook, and perhaps your altimeter, you should be able to get back to your starting point without difficulty.

Mark the route if necessary. When traveling in the forest, it is particularly unlikely that you will follow exactly the same path on your return as on your way in, unless the topography of the area is very distinct. For this reason, it is essential to use biodegradable markers such as paper, which will soon deteriorate without leaving a trace.

If you have a GPS receiver, take the time at the start of your trek to establish a waypoint or landmark. This may be possible at the road where you leave your car. If not, then at least read the UTM coordinates off the map and enter this location as a starting point. Then later, if necessary, you can establish a new position and ask the receiver to tell you the compass bearing to your starting point.

Remember to keep your map and compass handy as you travel in the forest. If you carry them in your pack, you will not use them as frequently as you should, since you will not want to stop frequently to remove your pack. If the route is difficult, with brush, fallen trees, or other obstacles to be climbed over and under, it is especially important that you not carry your compass with its lanyard around your neck, due to safety concerns. Your pocket is a far better place for it.

IN ALPINE AREAS

Many of the same suggestions offered above for forests also apply to alpine areas. First, find and follow a route using natural topographic features wherever possible. You can use ridges, gullies, streams, and other readily identifiable features as handrails. Even if the route appears to be obvious, pause now and then to look at the map and find your location, and observe the topographic features that you are using on your route. The sudden arrival of clouds may turn an obvious route into a challenging navigational problem. Mark your route on the map in pencil, perhaps even noting the time of arrival at various places along the route. Remember that you should be able to identify your position on the map as closely as possible at any point of your trip.

If you must deviate from natural topographic features, then use your compass to find the bearing that you will be following on the next leg of your trip. Make a note of this bearing in your notebook or on the map. If you have an altimeter, look at it frequently and follow your progress on the map. Ask yourself frequently what you would do if fog or clouds suddenly came in and obscured your view of the return route. How would you recognize key points at which you need to make crucial route changes? Should you be marking the route at such places?

In selecting the route, try to minimize the impact of your party on the terrain. Many alpine areas are particularly fragile. Some delicate plants, such as heather, grow only a fraction of an inch each season, and a few thoughtless bootprints may wipe out an entire season's growth. If there is any trail at all, use it to minimize your impact. In the absence of a trail, try to stick to rocks, scree, talus, or snow to avoid stomping on fragile vegetation. If you *must* travel over alpine growth, try to spread your party out to disperse your impact as much as possible.

Open alpine areas are excellent places to use GPS receivers. At every rest stop, and at important route changes, take the opportunity to turn your receiver on and obtain a satellite fix. Save these locations as waypoints. In the event that you get off route, you may be able to acquire a new position fix. Then your receiver will be able to tell you the bearing to any of your previously established waypoints.

ON SNOW AND GLACIERS

Routefinding on snow is usually straightforward. One advantage of traveling on snow is that wilderness travelers can pick their own route. The best route is usually that which follows the path of least resistance. Take the route that seems to make sense. Many times you can see your destination, and the route is straightforward. The shortest distance between two points is a straight line. Sometimes, however, the direct route is too steep for the party to ascend comfortably. This is where switchbacking comes in, just like on trails that gain elevation quickly. It may be beneficial for the party to make a few deliberate switchbacks to gain altitude instead of wearing the party out by attacking the slope head-on. Remember, while making your steps, kick them in as if you were making them for the party member with the shortest stride. It is easy for the long-strided individual to take shorter steps, but difficult for the shorter-strided individual to make longer steps. Also, when on snow, *always* be aware of potential avalanche conditions. If a slope has snow on it, then that slope has the possibility of sliding. Slopes with a grade of 50% to 100% (an angle of 30 degrees to 45 degrees) have the highest likelihood of sliding, so always be aware of the grade of the slope—not just the slope you are on, but also the slope above you. (Chapter 1 includes techniques for measuring the grade of a slope on a map, and chapter 2 explains the use of the clinometer for measuring the actual angle of a slope.)

Many times you can follow previous bootprints in the snow to find the proper route. Even if bootprints are several days old, an observant navigator can sometimes pick them out from the sun cups and still follow the route. Vague bootprints will sometimes have a uniform indentation and may have a distinct, subtle ring of dust in them. But it is still your responsibility to know your approximate location and direction at all times. A wilderness navigator who uses the excuse "It's not my fault that we're lost—I was following tracks!" needs to read this book again before venturing out on another trek.

Following a route that has been put in on a snowfield is usually academic: simply follow your bootprints back. But prints are rarely permanent and can degrade quickly under some conditions. Wind and newly fallen snow can obliterate tracks, sometimes only a few seconds after they are created. The sun, especially at higher altitudes, can also erase tracks. This can be particularly surprising on a summer day when you thought that your descent back down following your tracks would be a piece of cake, only to find on your return trip that your footprints have melted out and have become intermingled with existing sun cups. Fortunately for the wilderness traveler, with a little homework and a few navigational tools you will be able to find your way back.

The best tools for routefinding on snow are the map and compass. By taking bearings on an intermediate objective like a pass or a rock outcropping, you can navigate toward that objective even if clouds move in. If you write those compass bearings down, then on the return trip you can easily follow the back bearings for each consecutive leg and make it back. Remember, though, that if you have not done your homework and written down the bearings when you could see where to go, and then the clouds roll in and your footprints get obliterated, you may be in trouble. It may sound obvious, but you must use your map and compass (and pencil) when you can see the route to the destination so that when clouds obscure the route on the return, you can still find your way back.

Another tool for routefinding is the altimeter. The clouds have rolled in, and you press on until reaching what you think is the summit. But a quick check of the altimeter shows that you are 700 feet lower than the printed summit on the map (assuming a stable barometric pressure). A look at the map shows a false summit 500 feet lower than the true summit. It is likely that you have not quite made it yet.

Consider this situation: You come down from the summit but lose the descent route in the clouds. Your footsteps are gone and you have no wands. You remember that your camp is located at an elevation of 6500 feet. You descend to 6500 feet and your camp is nowhere to be seen. By traversing the slope *maintaining* that contour line you may eventually run into your camp. This technique should only be used in an emergency, since it is imperfect at best.

A GPS receiver can also be used on snow and in whiteouts. The GPS receiver can give you a pretty good idea of where you are, and where to go, but only if you have set the proper waypoints. By setting waypoints and entering in important positions, the receiver can guide you to your objective and back. On long trips, when conserving battery power is a concern, you can get the proper bearing to your destination from the GPS receiver, set that bearing on your compass, and then follow that bearing using your compass. If being a few hundred feet to the left or right of your intended line of travel is not a problem, then the GPS receiver will suit your needs. GPS technology is not yet accurate enough for you to bury a cache of food on a featureless snow slope, save the coordinates in the receiver, leave for a week, and expect to find the cache again.

WANDS

One of the most dependable ways to follow your route down an indistinct snowfield is to follow tall, thin stakes called wands. Think of a set of wands as a portable handrail that you place on the ascent. Most people make their own wands out of three-foot green bamboo sticks purchased at any gardening store. To make the wands more visible, cut a six-inch piece of brightly colored duct

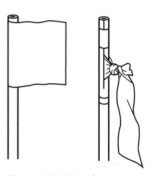

tape and make a flag at the top of the stick by folding the duct tape back over itself (fig. 27). Another method is to slit the first few inches of the bamboo stick and slip in a foot-long piece of plastic route-marking tape, then tape the slit closed. Wands made in this manner are sometimes torn apart in high winds, littering the slopes with pieces of plastic tape. We therefore prefer the duct tape method. Wands can be carried behind the compression straps of your pack, where you can reach

Figure 27. Wands

them for easy placement without removing your pack.

Placement of Wands

Wands are placed with the descent in mind. Place wands where they will be visible on the return trip. It is always better to place the wand on the top of a small rise than in a hollow. Beware of background features like rocks or trees which can cause the wand to blend in with its surroundings. Your wands should be as easy as possible to spot and follow. One helpful trick is to angle the wand slightly toward the previously placed wand. This way, when returning, if you cannot see the next wand, you will have a pretty good idea of the direction to the next wand. If you still cannot see the next wand, then have the party wait at the last placed wand and have a party member cautiously search for the next wand, always remaining in sight or within shouting distance of the rest of the party. Wait until you find the wand, then proceed to the next wand. It is all too easy for a party to rush down an indistinct snowslope and lose the wands under poor conditions. Once lost, it can be difficult to find the wanded trail again.

If the party is roped up, then a good rule of thumb is to place the wands no farther apart than the combined length of the rope teams. If the terrain does not warrant roping up, then the safety margin must be increased and the wands placed so that you can see at least one and preferably a second wand from each successive wand. It is easiest to find successive wands if they are placed at approximately equal intervals, so that you know where to look for them. This might require counting paces between wands to space them at predictable intervals. The party should always carry enough wands to make it to the destination. (The number of wands for each party to carry depends greatly on the length and complexity of the route. It is not uncommon for a party to carry one hundred wands for a long route. If you are in a party of four, that is only twenty-five wands per person.)

Wands left behind are considered litter. Always be sure to remove all your wands on the descent. Never remove someone else's wands; they are depending on them for their descent. Do not expect to follow somebody else's wands. They may remove them on the descent ahead of you, leaving you stranded. You and your party should be responsible for getting to the destination and back using your own resources.

It is possible that you may run out of wands before you reach your destination. Perhaps the conditions warrant more wands then you had anticipated. If this is the case, the party must decide a proper course of action. Perhaps you can use another form of navigation, such as taking a bearing from the last placed wand towards your known destination. Careful study of the map or an altimeter reading may help. Perhaps a GPS receiver can give some clues. (Remember that the GPS receiver is not a panacea. It is not accurate enough to indicate the position of your last placed wand.) Standing at the last placed wand in a whiteout close to your destination can be disheartening. In this situation one must be very careful. You have walked out onto the end of the proverbial plank. The prudent decision may be to follow your wands back down and try again some other day, and bring more wands next time!

GLACIER TRAVEL

The tools and techniques used for routefinding on snow can be used on glaciers as well. Generally, the route across a glacier follows the line with the fewest crevasses. Many times, just as on snow, a previous route can be followed. But often, especially if the route is old or if it is late in the season, the existing route will end at a gaping crevasse, the sign of a collapsed snow bridge. A new route will have to be made over or around the crevasse in order to continue.

Sometimes, if there is a crevasse that has just begun to show itself, a previous party may have placed two wands together forming an X. This is a warning to steer clear—a crevasse is probably looming underneath.

True routefinding on a glacier, that is, making a route where there was none, is an art and science. By using all of the tools of navigation (the map, compass, altimeter, pencil, brain, guidebooks, and experience), the learned wilderness traveler can safely and efficiently negotiate a rope team through the maze of crevasses on a glacier.

Always rope up on glaciers or on other snowfields where there is any possibility of crevasses. Most areas indicated on topographic maps as white with blue contour lines indicate glaciers (usually with crevasses) or permanent snowfields (usually without crevasses). If there is any ambiguity concerning which of these conditions is indicated, always assume it is a crevassed glacier and rope up, unless there is trustworthy information to the contrary from a knowledgeable source, such as a park or forest ranger or a guidebook.

THE BOOTPRINT

Every bootprint tells a story. Bootprints can tell you a lot about who and when someone has walked in the path before you. As you travel, pay attention to who is in front of you and what type of prints *you* are leaving. Pay attention to the size of the print, the shape of the sole, the style of the tread pattern, the depth of the print, and the direction of the print. Was the person who left those prints tall or short? Were they wearing a big, heavy pack, causing deep prints? Or were they wearing tennis shoes? Do you know what your own bootprint looks like? Could you follow it back after other people have made new prints on top of it?

How can you tell if you are the first travelers of the day on any particular route? Well, if the only prints that you see are facing you and look like they may have been made the previous day, then chances are that you are the only ones up there.

How far ahead is the next person? If the tracks that you are following are filling in with water from a puddle, then they are right around the corner. If the prints have fir needles or leaves on them, then they are older. If the tracks in the mud are drying and becoming less defined, then they must be at least a few hours ahead of you.

How are your teammates' energy levels doing? If someone is ahead of you and wearing crampons, then you can make very specific observations about their gait. Are there two long parallel streaks leading to the rear crampon marks? This may indicate a party member who is getting tired. The important point here is to be aware. Use all the information that is available, not just the obvious.

Once, a large group was ascending a trail. One member had to stop to make a clothing adjustment. He told everyone to continue on. One other experienced party member waited with him. The two began to follow after a few minutes. The trail began to be obscured by snow but the tracks from the party ahead were fresh and easy to follow. Then the tracks split into two different directions. Both sets of tracks were made at about the same time. (It was a popular route.) "Which way do we go?" the less experienced man said. The more experienced man knelt down and carefully examined the two paths, without disturbing them. He reached down and touched some of the prints, testing them and seeing how the snow had formed in the spaces between where the cleats of the boot had left the prints. "They went this way," the experienced man pointed. "How do you know?" the other man asked. The more experienced man explained that he had noticed that the last person in the group that they were following was a woman who was wearing the same style of boot that he was wearing, only it was about five sizes smaller. The odds of someone else having the same size and style of boot as that woman at that hour on that trail were low. Therefore, they went that way. All they needed to do was to follow those same prints. The two followed the unique prints and after a few minutes they caught up with the group. If the two of them had simply blundered along, unaware of the tracks that they were following, they most likely would have missed the group's turn and may have had to double back after not finding them. But because of experience and awareness, they were able to find the group with little trouble.

Know your own bootprint. And know the bootprints of other members of your party. You may not be able to pick out every step taken along the way, but chances are you will be able to discern between ascending and descending prints, and more importantly, any changes in the prints that you are following.

THE ART OF WILDERNESS ROUTEFINDING

Orientation and navigation are sciences which can easily be mastered by anyone who takes the time, and makes the effort, to learn map reading and the use of the compass and other navigational tools. Practice and time spent on these subjects will enable anyone to become proficient with them. Routefinding is different. It is an art.

Some individuals seem to be born with an innate gift for finding and following a route on trails, through the forest, in alpine regions, and on snow and glaciers. The natural abilities of such people can be greatly enhanced if they thoroughly learn the sciences of orientation and navigation, through mastery of the map, compass, and other tools. Such knowledge can enable a good routefinder to become a great one.

Some other people are not blessed with great natural ability in routefinding. But there is hope for them, too. Through study and practice, they can also become proficient in orientation and navigation, and can even become experts in the use of the map and compass, if they expend the time and effort required to do so. Then, with time and experience, they can also acquire much of the art of routefinding, particularly if they travel in the company of good routefinders, observing and learning as they do. Above all, there is no substitute for experience and practice.

We encourage you to reread and study this book carefully, learning the sciences of map reading, compass use, orientation and navigation, and possibly the use of other navigational tools. But this book is not enough. Repeated practice and considerable experience are necessary to thoroughly develop the skills and acquire the self-confidence that comes with repeated use of the principles described in this book. So go out into the wilderness and put the principles of *Wilderness Navigation* into practice—at first, perhaps, on good trails, then progressing to off-trail travel with ever-increasing routefinding challenges. Eventually, whether you are a natural-born routefinder or not, you can become thoroughly adept at map and compass use and will at least possess the knowledge and experience to avoid getting lost, and to recover gracefully from the experience if you ever do. And who knows: some day you might become a great routefinder, able to successfully navigate your way to any destination, solving all problems along the way, and make it back to your starting point with little difficulty or incident—because you planned it that way.

BIBLIOGRAPHY

PART 1: BOOKS ON MAPS, COMPASSES, ALTIMETERS, AND GPS

These books are only a few of the many books available covering the subject matter contained in *Wilderness Navigation*. These particular books are mentioned here because they are sources of some of the information for this book, or simply because they are good books on these subjects. Other fine books on these subjects, many of which are out of print and difficult to purchase, can be found in libraries.

Be Expert with Map and Compass: The Complete Orienteering Handbook, Bjorn Kjellstrom, Collier Books, 1994. Contains useful information on maps, compasses, and their use together, plus information on the sport of orienteering. Latest edition of a classic book on maps and compasses.

GPS Made Easy: Using Global Positioning Systems in the Outdoors, Lawrence Letham, The Mountaineers, 1998. Contains useful, practical instructions for using GPS receivers with UTM, latitude and longitude, and the UPS grid at the poles. Contains practical information not found in most GPS receiver instruction manuals (e.g., information on UTM).

The Land Navigation Handbook: The Sierra Club Guide to Map and Compass, W. S. Kals, Sierra Club Books, 1983. Basic, step-by-step instructions for using map and compass with a slightly modified "Silva" method. Includes direction of the slope, grade measurement, finding north with the stars in both hemispheres, and much more.

Maps and Compasses, Second Edition, Percy W. Blandford, TAB Books (division of McGraw-Hill, Inc.), 1992. Much detailed information on road maps, topographic maps, nautical charts, map reading, orienteering, compass use, and more.

Staying Found: The Complete Map and Compass Handbook, Second Edition, June Fleming, The Mountaineers, 1994. Orientation and navigation using the method of orienting the map. Also includes finding directions with an analog wristwatch and the sun, aligning your tent to catch the morning sun, navigating with children, and more.

PART 2: BOOKS ON OTHER
ASPECTS OF WILDERNESS TRAVEL

These books are recommended to readers of *Wilderness Navigation* because they contain material which is important to all wilderness travelers, such as avalanche safety, first aid and accident response, climbing and scrambling, crevasse rescue, and more.

The ABC of Avalanche Safety, Second Edition, E. R. LaChapelle, The Mountaineers, 1985. Quintessential text for the backcountry user who expects to encounter avalanche terrain.

Glacier Travel and Crevasse Rescue, Andy Selters, The Mountaineers, 1990.

Leave No Trace Skills and Ethics Series, National Outdoor Leadership School. Separate volumes cover various parts of the United States. For information call 1-800-332-4100.

Medicine for Mountaineering and Other Wilderness Activities, Fourth Edition, James A. Wilkerson, The Mountaineers, 1992. How to prevent and treat injuries and illnesses encountered in the mountain environment.

Mountaineering First Aid: A Guide to Accident Response and First Aid Care, Fourth Edition, Jan Carline and Martha Lentz, The Mountaineers, 1996. Covers specifics of backcountry first aid when 911 is not available. Details the seven steps of accident response.

Mountaineering: The Freedom of the Hills, Sixth Edition, Don Graydon and Kurt Hanson, eds., The Mountaineers, 1997. The complete book on wilderness travel. From boot selection to aid, ice, and expedition climbing techniques, this is the bible of the mountaineering crowd.

Northwest Mountain Weather: Understanding and Forecasting for the Backcountry User, Jeff Renner, The Mountaineers, 1992. Northwest meteorologist explains weather patterns and trends encountered in the mountain environment.

Winning the Avalanche Game, Wasatch Interpretive Association (Salt Lake City, Utah), 60-minute video, 1993. Informative, realistic, and lively discussion of avalanche terrain, how to minimize danger, and how to utilize avalanche beacons.

APPENDIX:
WILDERNESS NAVIGATION PRACTICE PROBLEMS

All of the problems and questions on each page are to be done with reference to the map on the facing page. For measuring and plotting bearings on the map, you should assume that the solid vertical lines are aligned with north and south. The answers to all of the problems and questions are given at the end of this appendix.

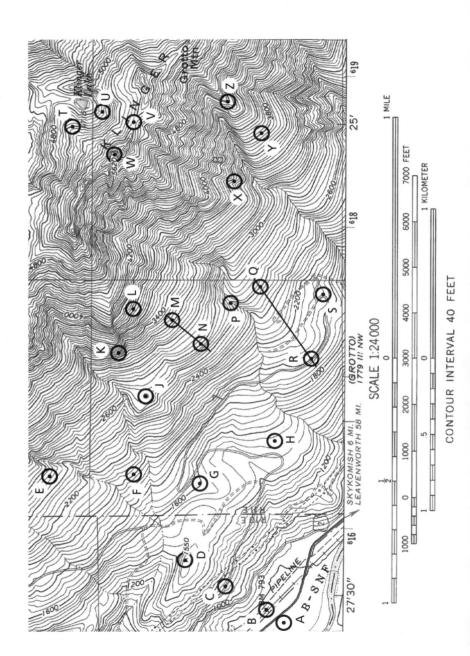

SCALE 1:24000

(GROTTO)
1779 III NW

SKYKOMISH 6 MI.
LEAVENWORTH 58 MI.

CONTOUR INTERVAL 40 FEET

Figure 28. Map to be used with questions 1 through 8 (*Illustration by J. Shontz*)

1. Name the general topographic features depicted at the following points:

A _____ D _____ H _____ K _____ L _____ P _____ U _____

V _____ Z _____

2. What is the straight-line distance from point J to point X?

_____ miles _____ feet _____ meters

3. What is the distance along the road from point C to point S?

_____ miles _____ feet _____ meters

4. What are the elevations, in feet, at each of the following points?

G _____ F _____ E _____ B _____ W _____

5. What is the grade of the slope between points N and M? _____

6. What is the grade of the slope between points R and Q? _____

7. What is the general direction of the slope (fall line) at point Y? _____

8. What is the bearing of the slope (fall line) at point T? _____

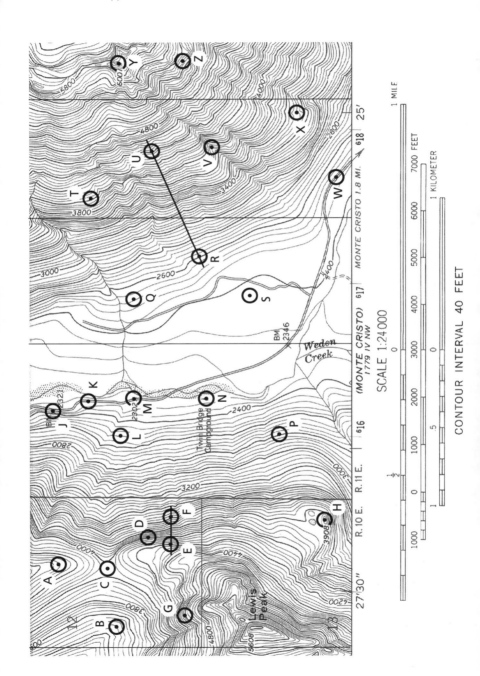

Figure 29. Map to be used with questions 9 through 16 (*Illustration by J. Shontz*)

9. Name the general topographic features depicted at the following points:

A _____ B _____ C _____ D _____ H _____ Q _____ S _____
V _____ Z _____

10. What is the straight-line distance from point *J* to point *N*?
_____ miles _____ feet _____ meters

11. What is the distance along the road from point *K* to point *W*?
_____ miles _____ feet _____ meters

12. What are the elevations, in feet, at each of the following points?
P _____ L _____ Y _____ X _____ M _____

13. What is the grade of the slope between points *R* and *U*? _____

14. What is the grade of the slope between points *E* and *F*? _____

15. What is the general direction of the slope (fall line) at point *G*? _____

16. What is the bearing of the slope (fall line) at point *T*? _____

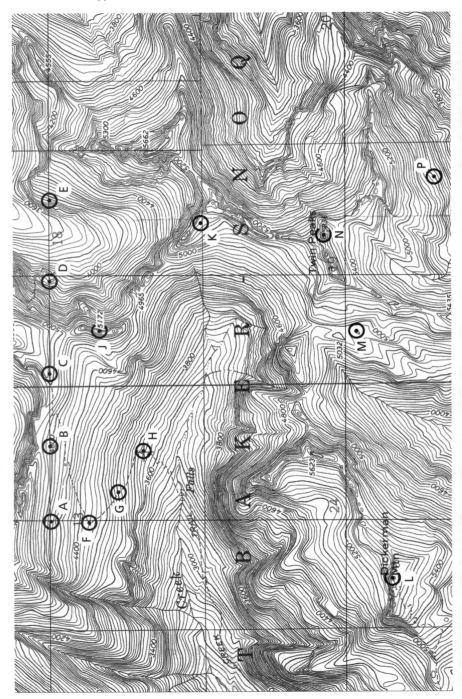

Figure 30. Map to be used with problems 17 through 23 *(Illustration by J. Shontz)*

17. What is the bearing from point *P* to point *M*? _____

18. Plot a bearing of 315 degrees from point *K*. Where does this plotted line intersect the horizontal line at the top of the map? _____

19. You are somewhere on this map, but you do not know exactly where. You take a bearing on the east peak of Twin Peaks (point *N*) and get 128 degrees. You then take a bearing on Dickerman Mtn. (point *L*) and get 207 degrees. Where are you? _____

20. You are hiking along the trail in the upper left portion of this map. You wish to find out exactly where you are. You take a bearing on Peak 5172 (point *J*) and get a bearing of 93 degrees. Where are you? _____

21. You are on the trail in the upper left part of this map. Your altimeter reads 4000 feet. Where are you? _____

22. From the east peak of Twin Peaks (point *N*), you descend to the northeast. At about what elevation do you expect to encounter a steep cliff? _____

23. From the summit of Peak 5172 (point *J*), you see a peak and take a bearing on it. You get 185 degrees. What is the approximate elevation of this peak? _____

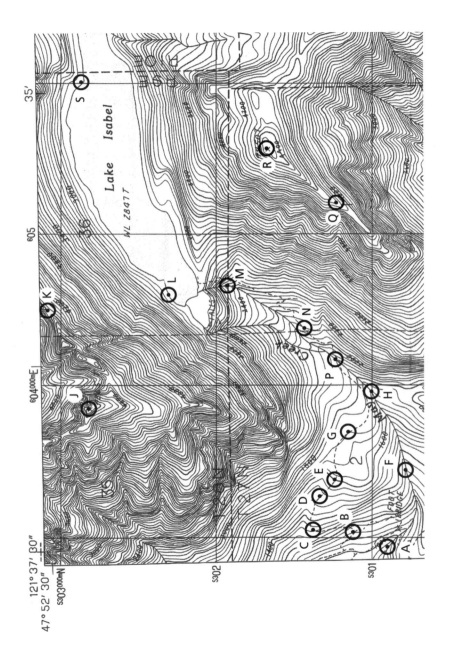

Figure 31. Map to be used with problems 24 through 30

24. What is the bearing from point S to point R? _____

25. You are along May Creek, but you do not know exactly where. You take a bearing on Peak 4450 (point R) and get 72 degrees. Where are you? (Indicate the letter closest to your position.) _____

26. You take a bearing on Peak 4450 (point R) and get 78 degrees. You take a bearing on Peak 4865 (point J) and get 17 degrees. Where are you? (Indicate the letter closest to your position.) _____

27. You are somewhere along May Creek. Your altimeter shows an elevation of 1320 feet. Where are you? (Indicate the letter closest to your position.) _____

28. Your intended destination is the pass at point K. You do not know your present position. You take a bearing on point R (Peak 4450) and get 159 degrees. You also take a bearing on point J (Peak 4865) and get 271 degrees. What bearing should you follow to get to point K? _____

29. You are in UTM Zone 10. You are at point L, and you turn on your GPS receiver. What is the approximate UTM reading of easting and northing that you should see on the GPS receiver? _____

30. Your intended destination is point Q. You wish to enter this as a waypoint on your GPS receiver. What UTM coordinates would you enter on the receiver? _____

ANSWERS TO PROBLEMS

1. *A:* Nearly flat area   *D:* Summit   *H:* Gentle slope   *K:* Cliff
   L: Steep slope   *P:* Gully   *U:* Bowl (amphitheater)
   V: Saddle or pass   *Z:* Ridge
2. 0.95 miles, 5000 feet, and 1500 meters (1.5 km)
3. 2.2 miles, 11,600 feet, and 3500 meters (3.5 km)
4. *G:* 1600 feet   *F:* 2000 feet   *E:* 2500 feet   *B:* 793 feet
   W: 5620 feet
5. Vertical = 400 feet. Horizontal = 800 feet.
   Grade = 400/800 = 0.50, or 50%
6. Vertical = 600 feet. Horizontal = 1900 feet.
   Grade = 600/1900 = 0.32, or 32%
7. General direction of slope (fall line) is southwest. This is the
   direction perpendicular to the contour lines at point *Y.*
8. Bearing of slope at point *T* is about 70 degrees.
9. *A:* Ridge   *B:* Bowl or amphitheater   *C:* Saddle or pass
   D: Cliff or very steep slope   *H:* Peak   *Q:* Gentle slope
   S: Flat area   *V:* Gully   *Z:* Steep slope
10. 0.6 miles, 3200 feet, and 960 meters (0.96 km)
11. 1.5 miles, 7900 feet, and 2400 meters (2.4 km)
12. *P:* 2800 feet   *L:* 2520 feet   *Y:* 6001 feet   *X:* 3500 feet
    M: 2302 feet
13. Vertical = 4400 - 2600 = 1800 feet. Horizontal = 2500 feet.
    Grade = 1800/2500 = 0.72, or 72% Note that this is the *average*
    slope between these two points. From 2600 feet to about 3400
    feet, it is gentler than a 72% grade. Between 3400 feet and 4400
    feet it is steeper than a 72% grade.
14. Vertical = 600 feet. Horizontal = 600 feet.
    Grade = 600/600 = 1.00, or 100%
15. General direction of slope (fall line) is northwest. This is the
    direction perpendicular to the contour lines at point *G.*
16. Bearing of slope at point *T* is about 240 degrees.
17. 296 degrees
18. Point *C*
19. Point *H,* at elevation 3720 feet along the trail, near a
    switchback
20. Point *F*
21. Point *G*
22. 4400 feet
23. 5240 feet
24. 199 degrees

25. Point P, where the trail crosses May Creek at an elevation of about 1900 feet
26. Point E on trail
27. Point F
28. 292 degrees
29. 10 6 04 600E; 53 02 300N
30. 10 6 05 200E; 53 01 200N (the latter number is 53 01 240N, rounded to the nearest 100 meters)

INDEX

ABOUT THE AUTHORS

A long-time member of The Mountaineers, Bob Burns has hiked, scrambled, climbed, and snowshoed extensively in Washington, Oregon, and California. He has been teaching classes in the use of map and compass since the late 1970s, not only for Club courses but also for search and rescue groups and local schools. The author, with the assistance of Mike Burns, of the "Navigation" chapter in *Mountaineering: The Freedom of the Hills*, 6th ed., he has also written articles on the use of GPS in wilderness travel (with Mike) and on leave-no-trace wilderness practices.

Mike Burns is a rock, ice, and expedition climber who has climbed in the Pacific Northwest, Colorado, Alaska, Canada, Mexico, Argentina, Nepal, and India, including a first ascent in the Himalaya. For the past five years he has been an instructor and lecturer on the technical aspects of climbing, including navigation. He has written numerous articles for *The Mountaineer* and *Climbing* Magazine.

THE MOUNTAINEERS, founded in 1906, is a nonprofit outdoor activity and conservation club, whose mission is "to explore, study, preserve, and enjoy the natural beauty of the outdoors. . . . " Based in Seattle, Washington, the club is now the third-largest such organization in the United States, with 15,000 members and five branches throughout Washington State.

The Mountaineers sponsors both classes and year-round outdoor activities in the Pacific Northwest, which include hiking, mountain climbing, ski-touring, snowshoeing, bicycling, camping, kayaking and canoeing, nature study, sailing, and adventure travel. The club's conservation division supports environmental causes through educational activities, sponsoring legislation, and presenting informational programs. All club activities are led by skilled, experienced volunteers, who are dedicated to promoting safe and responsible enjoyment and preservation of the outdoors.

If you would like to participate in these organized outdoor activities or the club's programs, consider a membership in The Mountaineers. For information and an application, write or call The Mountaineers, Club Headquarters, 300 Third Avenue West, Seattle, Washington 98119; (206) 284-6310.

The Mountaineers Books, an active, nonprofit publishing program of the club, produces guidebooks, instructional texts, historical works, natural history guides, and works on environmental conservation. All books produced by The Mountaineers are aimed at fulfilling the club's mission.

Send or call for our catalog of more than 300 outdoor titles:

The Mountaineers Books
1001 SW Klickitat Way, Suite 201
Seattle, WA 98134
1-800-553-4453
e-mail: mbooks@mountaineers.org
website: www.mountaineers.org

Other titles you may enjoy from The Mountaineers:

GPS MADE EASY: Using Global Positioning Systems in the Outdoors, Second Edition, *Lawrence Letham*
Thoroughly revised, bestselling guide to using a GPS receiver during all outdoor activities. Features extensive information on using GPS with maps and in rough terrain, using clear language and illustrations to demystify GPS.

STAYING FOUND: The Complete Map and Compass Handbook, Second Edition, *June Fleming*
Presents an easy-to-use map-and-compass system, with instruction on route planning and winter navigation.

SECRETS OF WARMTH: Never Be Cold Again, Second Edition, *Hal Weiss*
A comprehensive guide to planning ahead, choosing the correct materials, and using common sense to prevent hypothermia, covering emergencies in the wilderness, the city, at home, and in a stalled car in a freezing climate.

BACKPACKER'S EVERYDAY WISDOM: 1001 Expert Tips for Hikers, *Karen Berger*
Expert tips and tricks for hikers and backpackers selected from one of the most popular *BACKPACKER* Magazine columns. Covers everything from planning to emergency improvisations.

BACKPACKER'S WILDERNESS 911: A Step-by-Step Guide for Medical Emergencies and Improvised Care in the Backcountry, *Eric A. Weiss, M.D.*
A quick-access wilderness medicine guide featuring field improvisations from the experts at *BACKPACKER* Magazine.

BACKPACKER'S MAKING CAMP: A Complete Guide for Hikers, Mountain Bikers, Paddlers & Skiers, *Steve Howe, Alan Kesselheim, Dennis Coello, John Harlin*
A comprehensive, detailed camping how-to compiled by *BACKPACKER* Magazine field experts.

BACKPACKER'S LEAVE NO TRACE: A Guide to the New Wilderness Etiquette, *Annette McGivney*
A comprehensive guide to doable Leave No Trace techniques for all outdoor recreationists. Written by a contributing editor of *BACKPACKER* Magazine.

EMERGENCY SURVIVAL HANDBOOK, *American Outdoor Safety League*
Indexed information for fast response to medical emergencies.

HYPOTHERMIA, FROSTBITE, AND OTHER COLD INJURIES: Prevention, Recognition, Prehospital Treatment, *James A. Wilkerson, M.D.*
A detailed guide covering the signs and symptoms, solutions, and the prevention of cold injuries recommended by the experts.